FINDING EVER AFTER

"Dr. Paul's personal examples make this not only a great read, he also sets us up for some incredible insights that can enrich our own marriage. This a must-read if you are interested in growing your marriage."

—**David Stoop**, Ph.D.
Author, *Forgiving the Unforgivable*

Finding Ever After

DR. ROBERT S. PAUL
with Donna K. Wallace

BETHANY HOUSE PUBLISHERS
Minneapolis, Minnesota

Published by Bethany House Publishers
11400 Hampshire Avenue South
Bloomington, Minnesota 55438

Bethany House Publishers is a division of
Baker Publishing Group, Grand Rapids, Michigan.

Printed in the United States of America

ISBN-13: 978-0-7642-0411-1
ISBN-10: 0-7642-0411-4

Library of Congress Cataloging-in-Publication Data

Paul, Robert S.
    Finding ever after : a romantic adventure for her, and adventurous romance for him / Robert S. Paul with Donna K. Wallace.
        p.   cm.
    Summary: "Through story and practical advice, therapist Robert Paul helps couples connect as they discover their marriage can be full of fun, fascination, and freedom. Addressing the needs of both men and women in one book allows individual growth as well as understanding of their needs in concert with one another"—Provided by publisher.
        ISBN-13: 978-0-7642-0411-1 (hardcover : alk. paper)
        ISBN-10: 0-7642-0411-4 (hardcover : alk. paper)
        1. Marriage—Religious aspects—Christianity. I. Wallace, Donna K. II. Title.
    BV835.P38   2007
    248.8'44—dc22   2007011987

DEDICATION

This book is dedicated to our four incredible children: Christopher, Jessica, Rebecca, and Nathan. Your contribution to my life is immeasurable. You are each unique and amazing. I love you with all my heart, and I pray for the love stories you are each living on your own journey toward finding "Ever After."

Acknowledgments

First, thanks to my amazing wife, Jenni. Without you, none of this would be possible. You are the love of my life and my journeying partner. You have been an inspiration from the beginning, and there is no one in the world like you. Jenni, you are a testimony to the unbelievable creativity of our Lord. You have the most extraordinary mind, heart, stamina, and faith of anyone I've ever met. I owe you my life.

I would like to extend an enormous thanks to my friend and collaborator, Donna Wallace, who truly stayed the course and from the start has kept a bright vision of *Finding Ever After*. Donna, you brought endless creativity and energy, as well as a crucial and much-needed feminine perspective; your meticulous care and attention to detail were impeccable. Thank you for your unwillingness to settle, for your patience with me, and your awesome sense of humor that allowed us to laugh, even when the going was tough. To her family, James, Cierra, and Spenc, her comrades on the journey, I thank you as well.

To my dedicated and tireless team at National Institute of Marriage: Your commitment to a grand vision of great marriages is awesome. To my partner, Mark Pyatt: Your dedication to living out your faith boldly and with integrity is an ongoing source of strength and comfort to me. I can't imagine doing this without you. A special thanks to Dr. Bob Burbee and Christine Arnzen for spending hours brainstorming with me and always bringing your A-game to the table. Also, to the rest of the clinical team, Tricia Cunningham, Gary Bruegman, Dr. Brett Sparks, Dr. Jared Pingleton, Nathan and Jane Phillips, Dr. Shawn Stoever, Verlette Berndt, Pat McLean, Cindy Irwin, Fletch McClelland, Cynthia Nicholson, Teresa Phillips, and Monique Wells: You have each made a significant contribution to my life and this ministry. To the speaking team, Dr. Greg Smalley, Kris Pace, and Ted Cunningham. And to our support staff, Sheila, Shari, Sara, Abby, Cassie, Ellen, Joanne, Leslye, Sheri, and Angie: Your commitment to our team, the mission, and to the Lord is incredible and deeply appreciated.

To my agent, Lee Hough, who has skillfully guided me on this journey: Lee, your faith in me and this project has never wavered. Thank you for always being available and for continuing to steer me through uncharted waters.

Thanks to Kyle Duncan and the whole team at Bethany House. Kyle, your enthusiasm about *Finding Ever After* has been a breath of fresh air. I get that this is more than just a job for you, and I appreciate your interest in truly making a difference in this world.

To Donna's mother, Bobbie Ward, who after the sun had set spent long hours word-crafting and poring over the text, I give my special admiration and thanks.

To Jack Herschend and our Board of Directors, Dr. Greg Smalley, Michael Boerner, Dr. Gary Oliver, Gary Allen, Kris Pace, and Cary Summers: Thank you all for your generous contribution of time, commitment, and vision for our work and calling. Jack, thank you for being a mentor and friend. I never leave a conversation with you without feeling blessed.

To Dr. Gary Smalley: I treasure our friendship, and thank you for your unwavering support, encouragement, and promotion. I wouldn't have the countless opportunities I do to follow God's leading without the trail you blazed. You have opened doors for me with continual generosity. I hope my work will continue to bless you as yours does me.

Thanks also to our beautiful children and children-in-law, Chris and Amara, Jessica and Chris, Rebecca, and Nathan. I can't imagine life without you. I continue to learn so much from you and with you. Thanks for allowing me to be your dad, and for providing so many great memories and stories to share together and with anyone else interested.

Thanks to my parents, who have loved me and believed in me from the beginning. I never remember a day in my life when I questioned whether I was loved. I continue to learn from you and love you deeply.

Finally, thanks to my Father in heaven. You have given me an opportunity to have a part in the unfolding of your plan and purpose. I know that you can get along just fine without me, but thank you for not wanting to. I love you, and I know you love me.

DR. ROBERT S. PAUL, co-president of the National Institute of Marriage, is the primary innovator and creator of the Institute's highly acclaimed Marriage Intensive programs that have become world-renowned for their success in working with couples in crisis. He is coauthor of *The DNA of Relationships* and *The DNA of Relationships for Couples,* a popular speaker nationwide at professional conferences, and has been a guest on numerous radio and television shows. Bob received a master's degree from Georgia State University, and a diploma in Christian counseling and an honorary doctorate from Psychological Studies Institute. He is a licensed professional counselor, and a former professor at Evangel University, where he taught in the Biblical Studies and Psychology departments, specializing in marriage and family counseling, human sexuality, and the integration of faith into all areas of life. Bob and his wife, Jenni, have four children and live in Branson, Missouri.

To contact Dr. Robert S. Paul, or for more information on marriage counseling, conferences, or other products and services:

National Institute of Marriage
417-335-5882
www.nationalmarriage.com

DONNA K. WALLACE, MTS, president and founder of Mere Images, Inc., has coauthored and collaborated on fifteen inspirational and health-related books. Most recently she worked with Greg Smalley and Robert Paul on *The DNA of Relationships for Couples.*

.

table of CONTENTS

INTRODUCTION

We never tire of the epic tale of undying love between a man and a woman, spun with timeless threads of adventure and romance. Our imagination is captured by chronicles wrought with danger and uncertainty, where two lovers dare to encounter their greatest fears for the sake of the other. Why? *Theirs is a love worthy of gallant sacrifice, a story worth living.*

At first glance, such a relationship might sound like nothing more than fantasy, but I couldn't disagree more. What we've widely come to accept as mere fantasy is, in fact, our deepest reality. I believe we are all born with incalculable potential, and I have learned never to underestimate the power of the human heart.

Nevertheless, I listen daily as couples privately confess to finding themselves restless, bored, even trapped in a reality worlds apart from their dream marriage. Whether outwardly cynical or quietly resolved, disillusioned partners ask, "What's the point?" I'm saddened that so many feel bound to a commitment they can't define: "I made a promise . . . and now I will live in regret the rest of my life. I'll stay, but I'll never be happy."

We've learned that men and women are from different planets; we know why men can't remember and women can't forget; we're aware of the battle of every man and the desire of every woman; we've heard what she most craves and for what he most yearns. Couples are loaded with communication styles and love languages, yet their marriages still seem mundane—far too often devoid of passion and fascination. She's secretly aching for what may never be. He's trapped in boredom, fearing the day he might cave in to temptation or fail to feel at all. Or, flip the variables—maybe he's longing and she's impassive. Either way, there's loneliness and restlessness.

It doesn't have to be this way! I am absolutely confident of our research findings and our revolutionary approach to marriage in the areas of adventure and romance. Through working with the National Institute of Marriage, couples are not only astounded at their initial relational healing, they're also blown away by how exciting and natural it can be to grow together as they discover and enjoy fun, fascination, and freedom.

In *The DNA of Relationships for Couples,* Greg Smalley and I walked alongside four couples whose marriages, through their early hours of emergency first aid, seemed hopeless and irreparable. If your marriage is hurting badly, I recommend you first take a look at that book.[1] It shares the stories of husbands and wives, once mired in cycles of fear, who came to understand how to care for their marriage, who embraced the healing power of forgiveness, and who found miraculous hope as they pressed on toward the union of their dreams.

In moving toward finding *their* Ever After—discovering new life and seizing momentum toward ongoing happiness—those couples invested in learning how to fan sparks into flames that will continue to fill their marriages with romance and adventure. I hope you will be motivated and inspired to do the same. Why should we stop at being interested in "knowing how to hang in there"? We don't just want to know how to survive; we want to know how to go from where we are in order to *thrive.* How to make the ordinary *extraordinary!*

INTRODUCTION

Close-to-Home Stories

Our previous "DNA couples" are not presented in *Finding Ever After,* but my team and I have brainstormed new features to make this book unique from other nonfiction works. I'll invite you home with me to meet my wife, Jenni. I hope you will envision yourself sitting with us on the front porch, sharing and laughing long after the sun dips low in the sky.

One reason I turn primarily to my own story is that I'm passionate about the miracles God has in store for your marriage; I've experienced them personally in my own. I have traveled the path from misery and near-disaster to a life I wouldn't trade for *anything.*

The Foundational Element of Inspiration

We want you to discover with us what it means to be vitally alive together as husband and wife, jointly traversing uncharted territories instead of punching life's time clock or longing for the next available escape route. Have you ever wondered what it might look like for two hearts to be vulnerably and intimately joined, day by day becoming the full expression of God in our homes and in our world? I hope you will find your own blueprint within these pages. Our Creator is the author and finisher of *your* adventure and romance.

A Radical Spin on Dramatic Tension

What draws us back again and again to our favorite stories? Just as with marriage, dramatic tension is essential to rousing and sustaining our interest. Here we find the necessity and beauty of arousal, which arises when male and female differences spark at the connecting point—the point at which adventure and romance meet. Though it's intended to carry the fascination of a fairy tale, *Finding*

Ever After is not meant to be an oversimplification of or detour from reality but rather the full embrace of it. What follows is an intensity-filled voyage through the dramatic tension of masculine and feminine differences.

A Non-Stereotypical Perspective on Adventure and Romance

Our generation's perilous pace frequently convinces us that we don't have time for make-believe damsels in distress and made-up mavericks swooping down to vanquish foes against all odds. However, in the contemporary era, married life requires flexibility and creativity like never before. While much in Christian literature has endeavored to bring about our awakening to the wonder and beauty of divine reflections in the masculine and the feminine, men and women still seem to be finding themselves in opposite corners, without "the connecting piece."

I want to show you that missing piece. I will intentionally address "his" and "hers" emotions and concerns while showing men and women the power of their own story *in concert with one another.* Unique but inseparable, "his/hers" components validate and allow husband and wife their own individual discoveries of the inspired life. Only then are both partners free to arrive, together, at the true climax of their story.

Though men and women often approach life and love through different doors—sometimes called "orientations," as in men tend to be oriented toward adventure, women toward romance—my desire is not to define gender differences as much as to help identify or recognize individual strengths. While avoiding stereotypical extremes, my aim is to set up references for men and women *in general*—mainly for the ease of communicating ideas—while also validating those who *intensely* identify with non-stereotypical approaches to romance and adventure. (Women tend to be much more diverse in identity and social roles than men.) Because many readers will identify with traditional roles, the discussion here will follow traditional expectations. This in no way should be construed, for example, as an invalidation of women who gravitate toward adventure or of men who are more uniquely oriented toward romance.

Ever After: Starting Now

I have always been delighted at the prospect of a new day, a fresh try, one more start, with perhaps a bit of magic waiting somewhere behind the morning.

—J. B. Priestley

Your love story is now.

Do you seek adventure—to be challenged, empowered, thrilled? Welcome to the pursuit and capture of inspiration, freedom, exhilaration.

Do you dream of romance—to be desired, treasured, fulfilled? Welcome to the reframing of your story, the actualization of your longing, the coming-true of all you were created to be.

Your curiosity can be reawakened. You can learn how to become playmates. Watch your dreams come true with discovery and passion as you make finding Ever After your deepest, most profound reality.

Note: At the end of each chapter you will find questions for study and discussion. You can also find a leader's guide online at *www.nationalmarriage.com.*

Part **ONE**

CHAPTER 1

— INSPIRED —
Becoming Fully Alive

And gentlemen, the point of the story is not that they lived
happily ever after, but that they lived.
—*Ever After,* the movie

Unlike my wife, I'm a light sleeper. When our kids were little, it often took less energy for me to get up and tend to the crying baby than it did to wake Jenni. One early morning, at about 2:00, my dreams were invaded by the sound of rustling paper on the nightstand, followed by something jumping on, then off, my shoulder. I bolted straight up and instantly had the lamp on. Then, with one giant leap, I vaulted out of bed, slammed the bedroom door, grabbed my glasses, and flipped on the overhead light. My startled wife, now fully awake, blinked at me in bewilderment.

"Did you hear that, Jenni?!" I was now standing in the middle of the bed, doing a 180° surveillance. I'd broken into a cold sweat, my hair was standing on end—literally—and in a flash of self-conscious realization I knew I must look ridiculous. I tried to recover, giving what I hoped would seem like a bored yawn, and plopped down on the mound of covers. (So much for manly valor.)

"That was one *vivid* dream," I said, trying to keep my voice in a low register.

"Honey, I heard it too."

Oh, man.

Dazed, with hearts pounding, we began searching every inch of the room for the resolution of our bizarre mystery. I could still feel the imprint on my shoulder. My imagination ran wild. Whatever it was, it had no business being in my house, let alone my bed!

Adrenaline coursing through every vein, we looked under the bed, in the bed, in the bathroom, through the closet, behind every piece of furniture . . . and found nothing. After what seemed like an endless search, we collapsed across the now-stripped mattress. What *was* it? I'd slammed the door closed so fast that the uninvited guest couldn't possibly have gotten out. Or could it?

We decided we'd better check on the kids and search their rooms too. Again we found nothing; they were sleeping peacefully. Now fully awake and still without an answer, neither of us was going to be able to rest for a while. Deliberating on how to proceed, we were both perched at the top of the stairs, just looking at each other.

A sudden movement below caught our attention. From around the corner, at the bottom of the stairs, a little head popped out and stared, then just as quickly was gone. We both saw it. *"A squirrel!"* We barreled down the steps, laughing, not knowing what to do next.

After verifying that every door in the house was tightly closed and locked, we zeroed in on the rodent, who saw us coming and shot up the living room curtain. At seven feet up, its eyes looked as big as ours.

In a moment of sheer sleep-deprived brilliance, Jenni, in disheveled pajamas, took charge, bravely grabbed a five-gallon bucket, and became my very own wild-haired, barefooted Xena, Warrior Princess. She pulled the piano bench to the window, climbed up, and eased the trap toward the squirrel. Apparently in the middle of the night it makes perfect sense to think a bushy-tailed beast would step into a wide-mouthed bucket and remain calmly seated while being escorted to the front step and released into the great outdoors. Just before the capture of the prize, though, the feisty little intruder opened it wings, sailed across the room, and attached itself to the credenza.

One of us let out a startled yelp; to this day I'm claiming it was my wife. Our mouths hung agape; neither of us had ever before seen a flying squirrel. Well, on TV—nature shows, and of course, *Rocky & Bullwinkle* . . . but this was in our living room!

In the end, we yanked open both front and back doors to finalize our predawn sitcom. As we gave chase, Rocky alternated between running and dive-bombing before he navigated toward the back door and freedom.

We never found out how our castle was breached—we were just thankful we rallied to ward off the invading threat! Later, as we reflected back on our victorious adventure, shaking our heads in disbelief and hilarity, we were certain of one thing: *In those moments, Jen and I felt totally alive . . . together.* Through adrenaline rush, sensory overload, and the call to arms, everything around us had suddenly come into sharper focus. Even the colors were somehow more vivid.

Such seemingly random events that break through everyday mundane existence can feel like wakeup calls. Something about exhilarating experiences compels us to want more. Moments like these connect us to a deep-down awareness of who we are and what is possible for us as a couple. Even if our initial years together were wrought with difficulty, our private dreams remain tightly woven with hopes for a brighter tomorrow and a core-of-our-soul belief that love will conquer all. Regardless of whether we're in touch with it daily or almost never, at our ground zero *we long for a marriage filled with adventure and romance—our own version of Ever After.*

Sadly for most of us, hopes and dreams eventually fade into responsibilities and routine. Our day-to-day reality may not be all that bad, perhaps falling somewhere between "a little disappointing" and "entirely unfulfilling." Nevertheless, we venture forward, faithfully adjusting to whatever it takes to build and maintain the status quo.

For Jenni and I, so many circumstances over the years have seemed outside our control that we found ourselves looking forward to those special times (as with Rocky) when adventure and romance broke through the patterns of commerce and commute, children and chores. Periodically we'd reenergize ourselves by fondly remembering occasions when we succeeded in springing free of parallel existence and really, truly feeling alive. Yet something inside me has never been willing to settle for living from one random event to the next, waiting for destiny to surface haphazardly. Are arbitrary moments enough for you, or do you want more?

Inspiration: God's Animation

While visiting her parents' home one summer, Tara went out and lay on the old sun-bleached dock. The lake water barely rippled in the afternoon warmth. She closed her eyes and felt the gentle breeze through her hair as her thoughts drifted back over her relationship with Brad. She wondered at how her dreams had been snuffed out in the brief span of four years, three jobs, two children, and one husband. It was as if all the air had been deflated from her soul; she felt like a limp balloon. She cried out to God, "I hate my story—I want a new one!"

How many of us at times can relate? Our marriages have survived hailstorms and hurricanes, but we've yet to find that mythical castle beyond the clouds—we may feel we've merely settled into a musty little cabin just outside the evil witch's reach (for now). It's widely approximated that 50 percent of all marriages end in divorce, and the Christian community is not excluded. More devastating still is the finding by two renowned experts that of the remaining marriages, only 50 percent report being satisfied.[1] The numbers aren't so simple that we can apply them precisely, but could it really be that only about one in four marriages experiences happiness and satisfaction? What of the countless men and women tragically resigned, disillusioned, and feeling hopeless?

A lifeless union isn't only a devastation to those who feel trapped in it. A marriage without love negatively affects everyone close to it; estranged couples tear at the pages of family, community, and society, just as they ultimately break the heart of God. We at the National Institute of Marriage (NIM) meet daily with those who feel their relationships are dead or dying. Many come in desperation, hoping we can help them resurrect their partnership from the verge of permanent demise. Yet few dare to hope their love will ever feel vibrant and alive again. They grieve the loss of something precious and now gone, wishing again for the very days of passion that drew them willingly and wholeheartedly into lifelong commitment. Somewhere along the way, dreams were buried under a tombstone of lonely, frustrated sadness that made "happily ever after" a fairy-tale ending for someone else.

Ever After is *not* just a storybook romance. This is the dream within the heart of every young boy and girl, the purpose and destiny each one longs to undertake and fulfill. We want to be loved and treasured, to be lost in each other's eyes and to rest in each other's arms. When we experience a child's capacity to imagine, or when we watch young lovers enrapt in infatuation, we are reminded of how all-encompassing hopes and dreams can be. Though they may get tucked away, they never die. Ask a young-hearted old woman about her favorite childhood games or her lifelong passions, and her eyes will brighten; her gnarled hands become animated in the telling.

For many of us, over time, even-keeled stoicism or defeated resignation has caused us to judge earlier musings as youthful fancy. If our dreams seemed dashed and our hopes unfulfilled, we likely concluded we were silly for ever having them in the first place. We let them wither away, chastising ourselves for having been so foolish as to once have believed that dreams were meant to be fulfilled, that hope could become reality. *Without hope, we atrophy and diminish. Without dreams, we are no longer inspired.*

And without inspiration, we do not grow. When we originally took hold of our dreams—for life, for marriage, for *ever*—deep inside us was a divinely placed longing to be dynamic (not static), active (not passive), changing (not stagnant). We were made to be energized and vital. In a word, God created us with the desire, the passion, to be *inspired.*

We hear of inspiration in many contexts: "He's so inspiring," or "You'll be inspired by her testimony," or "I need inspiration to write this book." What is it we're communicating through such words? Generally, we're referring to feeling motivated to strive for new heights and to extend beyond average toward awesome, but our culture has mistakenly blended the words *inspiration* and *motivation* to the point that we use them synonymously. We find inspiration's beauty in many people and places and things and ideas, yet there's something even more basic and foundational to the phenomenon of inspiration. Because the Lord formed us with both capacity and desire for it, *inspiration is at the very core of our being; it's the essence of life.*

According to *Webster's Dictionary,* the word *inspire* means:

(1) [to] breathe or blow upon or into; (2) to draw air into the lungs; inhale; (3) to have an animating effect upon; especially to stimulate or impel to some creative or effective effort; (4) to cause, guide, communicate, or motivate as by divine or supernatural influence.[2]

Ultimately, inspiration is God's life-giving, essential *inbreathing* that enables and empowers us to embark fully on the adventure of life.

In fact, life itself is divinely brought into being and maintained through inspiration. An act of divine inspiration brings us to physical life: "The Lord God formed the man from the dust of the ground and breathed into his nostrils the breath of life, and the man became a living being" (Genesis 2:7). By divine inspiration we are also enlivened spiritually: "[Jesus] breathed on them and said, 'Receive the Holy Spirit'" (John 20:22).

Whether married or single, in order to live intimately and passionately we must (1) allow God to breathe into us the Breath of Life and then (2) continue to allow ourselves to be filled. Remember how Jesus said he came so that we would experience life fully? (See John 10:10.) Inspiration is innately essential to what he means. Because we were made in the image of a relational God, we can be confident that our loved ones and our relationships matter to him. Our Creator wants nothing less than that our relationships be a reflection of how we are meant to be—full of vitality, fully inspired.

The ache for Ever After stems from our inborn design to be enlivened, in our own journey first, and then in our marriage. Without inspiration we remain inanimate, still figures waiting for the fairy dust to blow across our pages so we can run and jump, laugh and cry. God's inbreathing—his life force—awakens and vitalizes us, giving passion physically, spiritually, and relationally. *Once inspired (brought to life), we become motivated to stay alive. The more alive (inspired) we feel, the more motivated we become to be more, do more, have more of all that life offers.* (From this point forward, when I speak of inspiration or being inspired, I'm referring to being and feeling fully alive.)

Usually when we feel uninspired, the core factor is that we've forgotten or neglected our first and true wellspring of motivation. When we've been trying to get air from another source, or when we've been holding our breath, we're understandably out of sorts— we've either been getting the wrong kind of air or we've developed a sort of life apnea.

To have healthy relationships, we must live healthy lives. To live healthy lives, we must rely for our very existence on the very Source of life. Before we can fully embark on our ultimate voyage of living and loving fully, we must breathe in deeply of our Maker's life force. As God's Holy Spirit continually blows into (inspires) our spirits, we are guided, taught, encouraged, and motivated by his supernatural power. Then we can *aspire*, like breathing out, to do great and mighty things. This rhythm of first receiving and then giving is the foundation of faith and the defining feature of a romantic adventure.

Oxygen to the Soul

If the fundamental desire to be vibrantly alive is as compelling as I'm suggesting, then understanding some of the dynamics of fully opening your windows for fresh air could prove useful to you. The following four ideas apply whether you rarely feel inspired or you're frequently inspired but want more of a good thing. Rather than steps to follow, consider these to be attitudes or postures that can help make a difference.

(1) Willingness

Many people, consciously or unconsciously, have their windows to inspiration locked tight or severely restricted by a lack of willingness. You may have succumbed to the belief that inspiration is only for others, or that it shows up only as a random occurrence. You may have even come to believe that somehow you're beyond the reach of God's power. If the air in your spiritual home seems stuffy, it may be that the window to your heart is closed.

Some of the most basic and exciting facets of the Christian faith rest on our Lord's being alive today. His loving us with an unwavering love, and his willingness to fill us to overflowing, are completely available as long as we are available to receive them. I'm not suggesting a fake-it-till-you-make-it kind of faith. I'm merely encouraging you to examine your heart and mind. If you're lacking faith in God's goodness and faithfulness, it's possible that woundedness and doubt are inhibiting you.

I'm also not implying that this comes without risk. Living fully can at times bring us face-to-face with our deepest fears or lead us to experiences that take us to the edge of our comfort zone. Please know I'd never encourage you to become relationally careless or to treat your heart as if it were made of steel. (Proverbs 4:23 instructs, "Above all else, guard your heart, for it is the wellspring of life.") Instead, the question is this: If you are confined and limited, do you want to stay there, or *are you willing to experience the full range of emotions and face the inevitable moments of life's uncertainties?*

(2) Receiving

The inspiration that leads to life is an unearned, unmerited gift from a loving Father to his children. We begin life with zero understanding about how to navigate our way, without any ability to fend for ourselves, and with little say about what goes on in our own lives. As we grow up, this situation changes dramatically; step by step we gain the ability to exercise our will and make choices. Life continues to be given as a gift, and *the older we get, the more important the choice to receive that gift becomes.* We can completely reject the gift by killing ourselves physically, but we can also reject it more subtly by not allowing God to fill us and to lead us in a meaningful expression of it.

(3) Remaining Available

The breath of God, and the fullness of his Spirit, is a continual filling of our physical and spiritual lungs—and then of the lives of those around us—as we inhale and exhale. I love the image of wind and its power (yet another illustration of God's inspiration) keeping us in motion, generating the energy we need to continue sailing on our way. As we're willing to allow for his movement in us, we raise our ship's sail and allow his power to snap it tight, propelling us forward. We may have quiet times when the air around us is so still it seems nonexistent, but if we want to be carried forward, *we need to make sure our sail is up and ready to catch the wind when it picks up again.* We must remain available.

(4) Inspiring Others

Being an inspiration to others has less to do with actively or consciously setting out to do something than with what results naturally from living an inspired life. If you take in a big gulp of air, what are you going to do with it? You exhale without even thinking about it. *Others are inspired when we live in rhythm with God;* they're drawn to him by experiencing the outflow of our being continually refilled and reenergized.

As you exhale the life of God, you become a motivation to those longing to feel inspired—others can't help experiencing the reality of your "Eternal Source." Just by being around you, they're around him, and as they realize where it's coming from, they too can turn toward him rather than looking only to you. Puts a whole new spin on evangelism, doesn't it? Rather than a duty we must fulfill, we are free to run, filled with hope and expectation, knowing others will follow. With this piece in place, the abundant life blesses you and fills you *and* becomes one of the greatest forms of blessing others.

Inspired Relationships

You might be tempted to think that I'm an unrealistic optimist, or maybe even a hopeless romantic. I'll admit I am a bit of both, but I am also a fierce realist. At NIM we run the equivalent of a marriage emergency room, and often work with the people that everyone, including the couples themselves, have all but given up on. And *because we daily witness the miraculous, we believe anything is possible.* Through our confidence in God's inspiration, we have one of the highest success rates in the business with couples in distress.

God is interested in the success of his children's lives and relationships; *we* merely help people get out of the way of obstructing his blessing. We try to follow the Creator's lead, knowing his desire for our lives to be full and satisfying, not in the absence, but in the midst, of inevitable hardships and challenges. Therein we've learned many valuable and powerful lessons, and the first of these is to open your heart as wide as possible to experience all that God has for you and your marriage.

I am passionate about these truths because I've seen them animated up close and personally. My marriage to Jenni is now twenty-six years old; the first half of those years was extremely trying and frequently painful for both of us. Just before our wedding, Jenni led me to Christ. She'd been a believer most of her life and, after a brief time of running in the wrong direction, was on a journey back with him. Through her influence, I was changed also, even though at first it didn't make our marriage easier. Radical faith didn't alter the fact that we both can be stubborn and opinionated.

And, as a newbie believer, I often didn't hesitate to give Jenni suggestions on improving her faith. However, while motivation can come from many sources, true inspiration comes from only One.

Even in the midst of frustration and disappointment, being able to watch my wife walk out her faith was absolutely inspiring to me. I saw evidence of God's hand working in ways I'd never before noticed. In fact, at times I saw him appearing in ways I didn't even know were possible.

You see, Jenni lives in the full belief that God is present, available, and entirely engaged in every aspect of her life. Her expectation is that when she speaks with God (which she does continually), he is right there listening and ultimately will respond in an obvious and notable way. Just as with any relationship, there may be periods of silence, but with him there are never periods of absence. Whether asking for help finding a parking place in a crowded lot (which I struggle with, concerned about bothering God with trivial details), prayerfully reading Scripture and fully expecting a response (either through the words on the page or directly to her heart), or awakening from a dream with the sense that God may have spoken to her through it, Jenni's relationship with God is as real as her relationship with me. Her heart is filled with love, and her desire is to stay intimately connected, serving her loving Savior in as many ways as she can, however he directs.

At first, I thought she was a little fanatical and naïve, but through up-close observance I began to witness happenings that were hard to explain away as mere coincidence. Plus, the volume of occurrences began to mount. Jenni was often hurt by my comments of disbelief and my belittling of her faith, but she was not swayed or crushed, and God began to get my attention. As a result of his working through her faithfulness, doors to my heart, mind, and spirit were opened that I didn't know I had—let alone had closed. *In the early years of my faith, I experienced God more through watching him interact with Jenni than I did in my own life.* As a result, I gradually became convinced I had grossly underestimated my Lord, and I became increasingly conscious of him with each breath I took.

Your marriage story is undoubtedly different than mine, but without question it's just as capable of being a motivation to fully live and be all you can be. Couples don't have to be two stellar individuals in order to motivate each other.

In the movie *As Good As It Gets,* Jack Nicholson's cantankerous character falls in love with a caring, patient waitress, played by Helen Hunt. The soft place in his heart is so small, or so concealed, that it's almost impossible to find.

Initially, he's nothing but abrasive and hurtful. And he only cares about her because she's the only person he wants waiting on his table. But he gives her something that exceeds what she's ever imagined. And even though the gift was motivated by self-interest, it changes her life.

Slowly and humorously, she begins to find a soft place in her heart for the obnoxious grump. One touching element is in how he labors to move beyond his obsessions and his rudeness to connect meaningfully (which he's been incapable of doing) to tell her how he feels about her. Yet just by being his normal self he continually upsets and wounds her.

When he injures her so deeply that she's on the edge of giving up on him for good, he has a moment of sudden clear sincerity. She has challenged him to say something nice about her—to give her an actual compliment. In his roundabout way, he ends up stopping her in her tracks.

> I have this—what? Ailment.... And my doctor—a shrink ... who I used to see all the time ... he says 50 or 60 percent of the time a pill can really help. I hate pills. Very dangerous things, pills.... My compliment is that when you came to my house that time ... the next morning I started taking these pills.

Confused, not seeing where he's going with this—what could

his psychotropic medication have to do with her?—she says, "I don't quite get how that's a compliment for me."

Uncharacteristically, he rises to the occasion, looks her in the eye, and says: *"You make me want to be a better man."* Now, that's inspiration! She motivated him to live more fully, just as Jenni motivated me.

Obstacles to the Inspired Life

Reality was such a jungle—no signposts, landmarks, or boundaries.
—Helen Hayes

If your marriage feels a bit risky at times, it might be fun. If it feels as though destruction is in your immediate future, yours is a different story altogether, and we'll get to that later. However, I meet spouses who don't want *anything* to shake up their world. They will avoid everything involving a hint of risk or a measure of newness. If this is true of your take on marriage, your life will be as predictable as this world will allow, but you likely won't be living with much zeal or inspiration. While several obstacles exist that hinder our ability to become and remain inspired, I want to focus here on three: fear, boredom, and the happily-ever-after fantasy.

Fear

We have no single greater enemy to inspiration than fear. Though fear can be extremely motivating, it is never inspiring. It serves a useful purpose, but one quite different than that of being animated and set free to thrive.

Fear arises out of something we perceive as a threat, either physically or emotionally. Fear motivates us to protect ourselves and survive. It often involves pulling in, hunkering down, squeezing our eyes closed, and holding our breath. Whether we're in fight mode or flight mode, our protective stance typically includes locking down our heart and spirit, limiting the extent to which anything, including God's breath, can enter. Remember that, in contrast, inspiration motivates us toward growing and expanding.

That sometimes people accomplish significant feats through a need to survive should not be overlooked. Even so, fear always keeps a person from being able to experience his or her fullest range of possibilities. Let me note here that I'm not only referring to fear as a reaction to or defense against being hurt (as when, for instance, facing a physical or emotional threat), but I also mean to include fear of failure, fear of not measuring up, fear of being controlled, fear of being rejected, fear of being powerless, and so on.

Fear's emotional responses range from mild to extreme. Fear can be a reaction to a threat so powerful it might lead a person to cower in a corner or retaliate in rage. I find that many of fear's more subtle forms are not recognized as such and go by names like *worry, anxiety, uncertainty,* and a host of others. The important point: Any of these states of alarm includes some form of pulling in, protecting, and an emotional or physical closing down—all of which hinders one's availability for openness to receiving an infilling from God.

Again, realize I'm not suggesting that fear itself can serve no purpose. Fear can be a dashboard indicator to help us recognize danger and then respond in moving toward safety. Overall though, fear, by nature, takes us in a direction that hinders the inspirational process.

Any relationship that includes much fear (worry, anxiety, uncertainty . . .) will struggle to grow and is likely to be unsatisfying to one person or the other, or both. A marriage will only flourish and become an exhilarating trek for both participants when it's based in safety and security. Marriage at its best is an openhearted experience where love and care are shared easily and liberally. Obviously, adventure and romance will include some measure of risk; if they didn't, marriage would quickly become routine. We'll discuss this aspect in much greater detail in chapter 6.

Boredom

A second rival of inspiration is boredom, complacency, and/or surrender to the mundane. Any time a person makes predictability such a necessity that there's no room for anything new, stimulating moments are unlikely to occur other than by accident. Yes, I just said that feeling safe and secure is essential to being postured for an inspired life, because a person who feels insecure tends to pull inward for safety. However, a person who succumbs to boredom also tends to shut down. The primary difference is that instead of withdrawing to self-protect, as with fear, a complacent person turns off and disengages.

Part of this mindset comes out of the prolonged and increasingly prevalent expectation that there will be nothing new, exciting, or interesting to learn or experience . . . so why bother? Boredom is best characterized by a yawn, a sign of someone preparing to shut down and sleep. Just as fear can bring a needful result, sleep has a useful function, but finding a healthy balance between engaging life and allowing time to rest and recharge is critical to living well and enjoying the journey.

As obstacles to living a fully inspired life, both fear and boredom are easily avoidable. (In chapter 3, we'll talk about preventing boredom from turning your marriage into a yawner.) Remaining engaged and interested is completely within reach, but there's one more obstacle to be addressed.

The Happily-Ever-After Fantasy

One subtle yet powerful way to knock the air out of a relationship results from an unfortunate byproduct of an innocent storyline imbedded within our cultural psyche. Children, young and old, love a good fairy tale. From "Once upon a time" onward we know that bad things will happen but that evil will soon be overcome by good. As the story reaches its climax, we feel assured that soon two lovers will be riding into the sunset to the tune of "and they all lived happily ever after."

We contentedly sigh, knowing all will be well from this moment on. The villain has been vanquished and all danger is past; the kingdom is safe once more. True love abounds between the handsome prince and the land's most beautiful woman. Theirs is a future of perfect peace and harmony, of continual bliss without fear or heartache or trouble. The adventure captured our attention and warmed our heart; completely satisfied, we're like a child ready to fall asleep.

We don't need a news flash to remind us that this is only storybook fantasy; we know escapist literature when we see it. And yet, believe it or not, to some degree all of us at times fall prey to the trap of a conscious or subconscious happily-ever-after fantasy. We often suffer great disillusionment when our story encounters the very kinds of serious struggles that were an integral part of the fairy tale and a normal part of maintaining an intimate relationship in a fallen world. Of course, we generally don't consider our own struggles "normal," and they certainly aren't fun. In our most difficult moments we can even feel as if we've been punched in the stomach and can't catch our breath.

Or perhaps your story simply has become boring and is presently more characterized by a continual yawn. In either case, we can reach a point where we look at how far our life and marriage is from what we'd hoped, and we see it as hopelessly flawed and want to trade it in for a new one. We want a real love story, not this poor excuse for a marriage! We know Prince Charming and Sleeping Beauty are pretend, but what about the affluent family up the hill, or the couple in church that seems to have the perfect everything? Their lives look so tantalizing. In a surprisingly short time our marriage can begin to lose inspiration.

You see, what so often gets people stumped is that they decide the saga they are living is not a real love story. When we encounter problems in our marriage, or when our marriage seems like it's becoming a dull disappointment, consciously or unconsciously, we generally find ourselves thinking, *Hey, this is not how it is supposed to be!* Whenever we entertain such a thought, we are (whether or not we realize it) comparing what we actually have to something else—to some sort of picture we'd previously painted in our minds. A fantasy.

Commonly, when our fantasy crashes against reality, we become deflated. As you continue reading you'll see that I'm in no way suggesting that having dreams for our future together is bad; in fact, you'll see the opposite. But who vividly imagines difficulties and hardships when they dream about tomorrow? Because of what we *do* envision, those realities generally catch us by surprise and contrast with our hopes and expectations.

Here's the thing: If your relationship experiences the types of twists and turns listed above, it has all the makings of a true love story! Have you ever considered that the challenges in life and the journey toward overcoming them are some of the very elements that make a story intriguing and adventurous? Every great love story is riddled with danger and nerve-racking "Fire Swamp" moments (as seen in *The Princess Bride*). What captures our interest is how daring and devotion carry the two lovers through all the perils besetting them. It's here that we see the strength of their characters revealed. We're fascinated by how their encounters with risk and conflict develop their passion.

Unfortunately, what causes many to jump ship just before the big triumph is not being able to see the big picture. When we encounter trials and challenges that look altogether hopeless, we allow our hope of finding Ever After to die. We fear nearing our story's climax and instead of hearing "They lived happily ever after," our tragedy closes with "The End" rolling up the screen. We don't realize we are not at the end of the story, even though from our limited viewpoint we see no way for the hero and heroine even to survive, let alone find Ever After.

One example of this is found in taking a child to the theater. About a half hour into the movie, Hero faces his big challenge—the point of no return—and it looks as if this will be the end. The child, fully caught in the drama, looks at you with pleading eyes, hoping you can do or say something to save the day. You nod, pull him in close, and say, "Let's keep watching to see what happens next." You don't flinch; you look down at your watch and see that only thirty minutes have elapsed. Of course Hero can't die yet; there's still an hour left!

We're often like the little child at the movies. From our limited perspective, life's circumstances look insurmountable, and we fear this truly might be the end. Unless we stay tuned in, we're likely to miss the best part, the big miracle. The key is recognizing that you're a major player in this drama; yours is a true, *bona fide* love story, one that God himself is writing with both of you specifically in mind as the star characters.

I too am interested in finding Ever After, but it's the real one I desire, not a Hollywood edition. As a believer in Christ I look forward to eternity in heaven—the *ultimate* Ever After. But have you noticed how even our thoughts of heaven can sound somewhat fairy-taleish? I don't know exactly what roles we'll have in the life hereafter, but I imagine we'll do more than sit around our "mansion just over the hilltop," watching angels for entertainment. I expect that heaven is far more enchanting and adventurous than anything we *can* imagine! One day our Prince will come and we will be swept away. In the meantime, I don't have to wait for a dramatic and spectacular love story to begin in my life, and you don't either.

As a living, breathing human being, I've already begun to live my Ever After right here, even in the midst of a crazy, messed-up world. My life and marriage have all the elements of a real love story: passion, love, romance, challenge, uncertainty, victory, tragedy, and more. Despite all the many hardships and difficulties, my hope resides in God's deep desire for my overall well-being and for the success of my relationships *now*.

Paul's prayer in Ephesians is that we will be "filled to the measure of all the fullness of God" (3:19). With Christ's help and involvement, I can begin experiencing more and more of the real Ever After from the very beginnings of infatuation. What about you? When was the last time you felt genuinely inspired in your marriage? If you don't like the way your story has turned out so far, or if you simply want more of a good thing, you have a golden opportunity. We all have the ability to collaborate with God in writing the rest of our story to include all the romance and adventure our hearts could possibly desire. So much so that when we enter our eternal Ever After, even we will look back at our own story and say, "*That* was an amazing journey!"

Conclusion

This book is not for everyone. It's written for those not content to survive or get by in life or in marriage. I welcome anyone who's willing to do whatever it takes to awaken to all that God has to offer. This will at times take you to the edge of and beyond what feels comfortable, predictable, or common.

We can intentionally choose to welcome and embrace God's creative work in us as a daily part of life. I'm excited about my eternal Ever After in heaven, but something inside me is unwilling to wait until I die to live fully. I invite you to believe with me that we can begin finding Ever After now.

What does it mean to be fully alive together as husband and wife across a lifetime? The first secret to having an inspired marriage is to recognize the two essential components of a life fully lived: the adventurous journey out into the world, and the inward romantic journey of knowing and being known. Both are fraught with difficulty and challenge because we live in a fallen world and because as men and women we tend to approach life and relationships differently. However, discovering how to embrace each other at the point of contact, despite all obstacles, is far easier than you might think.

God's desire for us is not to merely experience random moments of excitement but to embark on an incredible journey wherein his breath fills our sails and enlivens our soul. There is, of course, a natural ebb and flow to exhilaration. An inspired individual is a person in motion to the fullest expression of who he or she was created to be, engaged in the adventure of life and available to be motivated by and to motivate others to really live and become fully inspired. What does it look like for two hearts to be open, intimate, becoming the full expression of God? God is not only for our marriages, he desires to be fully expressed through us *together:* creating, ruling, and setting people free.

———————— *to* Ponder *and* Discuss ————————

1. Describe a time in which you and your spouse felt exhilarated and alive by an experience together.

2. Discuss the difference between *inspiration* defined as "fully alive" versus "being motivated."

3. What did your *"Ever After"* dream look like as a boy or girl? How has it changed?

4. How do you see faith playing a role in a romantic adventure?

5. What makes a story or a movie a great love story in your eyes?

6. Can you see your marriage having any of the elements of a great love story? What does the love story God is writing with you and your spouse look like to this point?

7. Share with your spouse what you think might be holding you back from embracing an inspiring love story with him/her.

CHAPTER 2

— ENGAGED —
*Embracing the Heart
of Adventure*

*To understand the heart and mind of a person, look not at
what he has already achieved, but at what he aspires to do.*
— Kahlil Gibran

Newly wed, we set out together toward the horizon of our future.
The sun is just coming up over the trees. The dew of morning spar-
kles on the leaves. Inspired and fully alive, we embark on our very
own love story. We know the dismal stats on divorce, but *we're*
going to beat the odds. Our marriage is not like the others; it's
going to last! We're going to make it. We may or may not change
the world, but our little family will always be a warm, cozy refuge
of its own, one in which love conquers all. The world's harsh

realities may give us their best shot, but we will weather the storm by pulling together, energized and protected by our love.

No one enters marriage expecting it to become a heart-wrenching drama.

The other day a friend of mine shared that she and her husband had sat down to discuss whether or not they should refinance their house. What seemed at first to be a simple chat about numbers soon progressed to a complicated discussion of where they planned to be in five, ten, fifteen years. He was getting more quiet and sullen as she pressed in with questions about his dreams for the future. Finally he abandoned all caution and, with a distant look, said, "If I pursued my dreams, the kids and the house would have to go." Stung by his words, she realized that he felt ultimately compromised and unfulfilled. Why wasn't their family life part of his dream?

Somewhere along the way this man had felt compelled to abandon his quest for adventure in exchange for a story that felt more responsible. His hopes and dreams weren't wrong; like all of us, his deep longings were divinely placed in him by his Creator. But that's not all. At the moment of our birth we are written into the pages of a wondrous love story, one which, like all great love stories, happens to be an adventure of epic proportions. We were created as an integral part of this tale that is, at its very least, meant to leave a mark on this world.

Our marriages are meant to become the magnificent centerpiece in that adventure. However, if our hearts were designed for Ever After, as God truly wants them to be, why is the path so elusive? Once again, the problem is not that having such hopes and dreams for the future is wrong. Our plight begins when we judge our journey, the one we're already on, as illegitimate and flawed because it doesn't match the picture we'd painted in our minds.

Finding Your True Ever After Adventure

*Courage is not the absence of fear, but rather the judgment that
something else is more important than fear.*
—Ambrose Redmoon

What makes a story an authentic love story and not just another fanciful notion? What makes it an adventure worth living? Think about the people you know whose story leaves a lasting impression and captures your interest. How about a gripping movie or novel that keeps your attention locked in and won't let go until the final scene? I guarantee it's not a scene occurring *after* the phrase "and they all lived happily ever after." How interesting can it be to live day after day without a care or a challenge? Who wants to live in the predictable black-and-white world of *Pleasantville*? A compelling love story is one that includes all the twists and turns, all the suspense that accompanies danger and intrigue—all the elements of real life.

Wild Fire

I don't care much for roller coasters anymore. I used to love them, but now anything that artificially lodges my stomach in my throat doesn't hold great appeal. Yet fate is against me on this. Silver Dollar City, our world-class amusement park in Branson, Missouri, continues to develop a new death-defying experience about every other year. When skillful advertising that promises the adventure of a lifetime is coupled with thrilling memories of yesteryear *and* a teenage son begging me to go, I'm a sittin' duck. I find myself saying, "Okay, just once."

Each year I'm just curious enough to give in to the newest, tallest, fastest coaster on the planet. I admit there might be a little ego involved too; there's never a day I want my kids calling their ol' dad a wimp for not showing adequate bravado. Last year the new ride was aptly named "Wild Fire." It begins with an enormous free-fall, plummeting straight down, dropping off the edge with zero gravity, followed by two tight corkscrews and two loop-the-loops— all within a few seconds of shooting toward the ground once more before careening to an abrupt, jaw-cracking stop.

I survived. Was it thrilling? Yes. Nate, of course, rode eleven straight times. It just wasn't fun . . . for me. Once I was locked in, I knew I had to endure it, and I knew I'd live through it, but I spent the next twenty minutes sprawled on a bench, waiting for waves of nausea to subside. Though I managed not to lose my lunch, this definitely isn't the way I want to do life. If I had to ride Wild Fire every time I went to the amusement park, I'd never want to go again.

I don't prefer white-knuckling it at Silver Dollar City, and I don't prefer it in my marriage. I'm always up for a good adventure, but I either need to enjoy it *or* it had better be for a good reason!

The Road Less Traveled, M. Scott Peck's bestseller, opens with the line, "Life is difficult." Peck spelled out what we've always known but don't always want to accept as true: Life will most assuredly include genuine heartbreak and tragedy, and at times it can feel like an out-of-control roller coaster. Nevertheless, it will also include breakthrough moments that lead to victory and success. Unfeigned love stories push the outer limits, but they must also have moments of passion and intimacy as well as times of peace, satisfaction, and harmony. Inevitably, the characters involved will learn and be changed along the way. One of my most basic beliefs is that my life is not a random event but was orchestrated by God on purpose, with purpose. While reflecting the love of Christ and with trust in his ultimate goodness, a real love story will be filled with meaning.

Adventure is an outward journey, pulling us and extending us out into the world, impacting everything around us. Something deep inside each of us cries out to make a lasting difference, to live a life that matters. It may be an adventure that changes the whole world or, for most of us, an adventure that starts with us and primarily benefits those closest to us. It need not be high-profile or well known, it just has to *matter.*

When thinking about a life filled with adventure, people do frequently envision a death-defying "Wild Fire" quest—something action-packed, with chills and thrills, shouts and screams. Those things can be part of the experience; however, if that's what first comes to mind when you think of *adventure,* I want to challenge you to broaden your definition. *Something qualifies as adventure if it simply involves an element of risk.*

Most of us already come face-to-face with uncertainty. Life generally and marriage specifically *will* lead us to places beyond our comfort zone. In fact, the quest God has you on might not even require you to do anything differently than you're currently doing. Or, it might. The point is, if you're willing to fully engage the life you've been given, there will be plenty of intrigue to make the journey interesting. The issue isn't whether you find adventure in something that seems high-flying or in something that seems mundane. *The important question is the "why" behind what you do.*

Some stunts, like bungee jumping, can be enjoyed without any particular aim beyond the experience itself. Rock climbing can lead to a profound sense of individual accomplishment without necessarily centering on another person and without focusing on making a difference. Adventure in and of itself is not bad or counterfeit; it's just that all by themselves, individual feats of strength and courage don't satisfy the deeper need for a life that matters. Our need for purpose and meaning must be attached to something significant enough to make all of life's challenges worthwhile.

We long to feel significant and to see our life as an integral piece of the puzzle. And we are. When that piece is missing, no matter how beautiful the picture, the puzzle has a gaping hole. In order to fully discover our place in the adventure, we must grasp what our life and marriage is actually all about—we need to know what it is we're trying to accomplish. Generally it will be a cause worth living for, probably worth dying for, and certainly worthy of your life's energy. So what *is* worthy of such investment?

In reality, people often miss what qualifies as meaningful. We're commonly impressed with the "big deal," and while we may not be thinking we need to be Billy Graham, we still believe our contribution needs to be publicly noteworthy. Many of us need to have our concept of what makes something worthwhile in God's kingdom challenged. In the end, fanfare and recognition are completely irrelevant. A smile and silent nod of approval from the Lord are all that's required to qualify. The adventure to make a difference in the world is the adventure of faith—faithfully walking with God and seeking to be more like him. It may include a public ministry, but it may also be a life lived with love and integrity in all of our interactions and relationships. The world may take note, or no one but God may notice. Our attitude and heart's desire to bless the world through our life and efforts may be sufficient.

There's a story Jesus tells of a widow with phenomenal faith; it moved him so deeply he used it as an example to all. The act of great significance was her placing in the offering plate two pennies—all she had. She had no way of knowing her gift would affect dozens of generations to come as an example of commitment to God, because it wasn't given for that purpose. I only hope she knew it touched the heart of her Lord and was meaningful for that reason alone.

The motive or reason behind what we do is as important as the act itself. When I felt a calling to serve God, I also sensed a word of caution in preparing my heart for ministry. I was encouraged to faithfully serve the Lord with all of my heart, soul, mind, and strength, but to be prepared to have a ministry like Jeremiah. At first that sounded horrible because Jeremiah was the weeping prophet; his ministry was to a broken and downtrodden people. There was little celebration and minimal public success associated with his calling. But he served loyally with love and compassion. Things haven't turned out that way for me thus far, but I must remain prepared to serve wholeheartedly with or without success or recognition. I constantly pray I am not a fair-weather servant, only faithful when things go well.

So remember: You were created on purpose, with purpose, but your reason for being might not be exactly what you expect. Fully engaging the adventure in which you've been placed could be as simple as faithfully loving and caring for your spouse and children, assisting them in finding their way with the Lord while supporting and encouraging them on their journey. It may be as a greeter at your church, warmly welcoming people as they arrive, giving them a firsthand experience of Christ's love through you. The options and opportunities are virtually unlimited; the key is whether you sense the Lord guiding, exhorting, and empowering you. Two pennies can impact the world for centuries—let the Holy Spirit define for you what's significant and meaningful, and don't be too quick to minimize the little things.

The Life and Times of Bob

Most people aren't privy to the fact that I am a two-time dropout. I went to college the first time right out of high school and lasted two quarters. Clearly I wasn't ready. I then spent some time as a musician in Northern California before heading back to college four years later. I still wasn't ready, but at least this time I met Jenni.

We got married, and shortly thereafter I began my journey with God. During those early years I had many jobs: musician, preschool teacher, furniture mover, waiter, shoe salesman, phone solicitor, car salesman, and stockbroker, to name a few. I was having a little trouble figuring out what I wanted to do when I grew up!

Overall, things were good. My marriage was tough, but I seemed to be making progress in life. The bills generally got paid, and my life was filled with as much success and as many good times as I could manage. I also had a growing awareness that God was at work doing something in me.

At one point, while I was selling cars in Los Angeles, my father asked me a question that began to gnaw at me over the next several years. He asked if I felt good about my life and work. Did I feel as if I was investing myself and my energy into something that felt meaningful to me—something that made my life feel as if it all made sense?

I don't remember how I answered, but I recall feeling uneasy about it. At that time I had two small children, and providing for my family seemed the most important thing I could do. I did eventually become dissatisfied as a salesman, and when an opportunity presented itself that included leaving crowded L.A. and moving my family up the coast, I made a change. I hoped this was my answer; a step up in career (becoming a stockbroker) and a move to a gorgeous location (Santa Barbara) seemed ideal and would surely make life meaningful . . . but as time went on, something was still missing.

Santa Barbara *was* awesome, and my job was fine. But it still felt like only a job. Meanwhile, even though I was active in church and various ministries, which all felt good and useful, I was restless. I knew there were ways to make a lasting difference within *any* chosen career. For instance, I had a buddy, Tim, who was also a broker and a strong man of faith. He invested daily in people's lives, and he used his work in financial planning to minister to them around issues of stewardship. I enjoyed seeing his passion, feeling his enthusiasm, and hearing his stories, but brokering never gave me the same sense of meaning and purpose. I never felt inspired by it.

———

My dad's question had taken root and started to grow. I not only knew I could somehow make a more significant difference with my life, I also really wanted to. Deep down I knew there had to be an *ultimate* reason for my being on earth beyond paying bills, seeking personal happiness, launching the kids, retiring, then dying and eventually being forgotten. I'd watch movies like *Braveheart* and be stirred by seeing a man whose life was driven by a *noble cause.* There it was—I was starting to see what was missing! Without it, especially on the tough days, I'd find myself asking, "If this is all there is, why bother?" Without a noble cause, sometimes life seemed too hard and generally senseless.

Finally the day came when the urging within me grew strong enough to muster the courage to step out in faith. I was finally ready to enter my adventure *fully* and allow the Lord to take me wherever he saw fit. I sensed a strong call to the ministry of counseling; in fact, I'd always leaned in that direction. Both my failed attempts at college were as a psychology major.

I wondered why I hadn't been able to stick with it, if this was what I was called to do. Each time I'd reached a point where I couldn't imagine listening to people's problems all day, every day. This time was different. I began to see the whole profession in a new light, including a different angle on what counseling is. My focus shifted away from listening to people drone on about their predicaments and onto coming alongside to empower and assist those who, like me, were longing and searching for something more. Eight years after I left school the second time, I invited my wife and kids on an adventure to follow God's leading. I wanted to go back to college.

Jenni and I prayed about it, and when she too sensed God's leading, we packed up the car and did the opposite of the Beverly Hillbillies, moving from Southern California *to* the Ozarks. People thought we were nuts, but the last two decades have been amazing: The journey has never been straight or predictable, but what a tale it's been!

Fortunately, through working with thousands of people, I've learned that following God and engaging in adventure doesn't necessarily require the kinds of radical changes Jenni and I made. Go ahead and breathe that sigh of relief, but make sure you don't miss the importance of discovering, together with your family, your own tailor-made potential. We need to take the time to consider the important purpose of our marriage in God's kingdom. Without a clear sense of what we're aiming for, all we sometimes see is meaningless daily hassles or the routine and conflict inherent in family relationships.

Once we are born, we're right smack in the middle of our adventure. It's typically not the one we asked for, it may not even be one we prefer, but here we are nonetheless. God created this world, and we Christians believe he is at work bringing about his plan. Whether or not we see it, we can trust that we are right in the thick of all he's directing. We have the option to be consciously involved, or not; we can either work with God or against him. This is where we are. Because I know this, I know everything I do and every aspect of my life in some way relates to the bigger picture of his unfolding plan.

I found myself asking why God would want my involvement, and whether he would be disappointed if I didn't engage in the work with him. What I then realized is that *my Creator made room specifically for me in his plan for my sake, not his.* God can get along fine without me, but without him my life is ultimately meaningless. It is only when I jump into the fray with him that I have hope of finding a reason for being that can satisfy my soul and bring complete fulfillment.

Therefore, God's disappointment when I don't participate is more like that of a father whose heart breaks for a child who's floundering. His desire appears to be for me to join the family business, not because he needs my help but because he wants to share the blessing. The adventure is bigger and more complex than I can fully appreciate, but I'm clear that whatever God is working out is significant, and I'm honored to be part of it.

In marriage we also have the option to link arms with God. There isn't one area of life that doesn't in some way impact what's going on in the kingdom, which is God's plan for us here on earth. Marriage is most definitely part of the design. Before we're able to grasp the full significance of our marriage, it helps us to first connect to the purpose of our personal journey. From there we can discover how our path connects with that of our spouse, and then how both can intersect and weave together into the divinely inspired adventure we call marriage.

Engaging the Adventurer

It is vain to say that human beings ought to be satisfied with tranquility: they must have action; and they will make it if they cannot find it.
—Charlotte Brontë

All of us are designed with a desire to accomplish or create something lasting and magnificent. We want to conquer, to overcome, and to be a winner, even though winning may be broadly defined in expression. The adventurer in each of us is drawn to being on the victorious side in the classic battle of good's triumph over evil.

This is true for everyone, male or female, but it's particularly compelling for men.

Men typically lead with adventure—what I call *the outward journey*. Most little boys (including older ones) want to feel like and be seen as a hero, especially to the people they most love and value. In fact, adventure is the doorway through which men enter the intimate world of marriage. As much as the adventurer exists also in little girls (including older ones), they are usually motivated toward adventure for reasons other than being seen as the heroine. Though men love the idea of experiencing lasting romance (see chapter 3), "romance for him" is inseparable from the adventure. Men, in general, approach relationships needing to be victor of the conquest. They long to be inspired through love and to be an inspiration to others. Men desire to have a life centered around romance, but most often they want it to be an *adventurous* romance.

Adventurers are driven deep in their souls to find the true reason for their being. Many men at some point give up on the idea of ever achieving their own hero greatness, but nevertheless are still drawn to it. Even if we've lost faith in accomplishing anything of lasting value, we'll find some way to experience the thrill, even if it means through spectator sports. Watching competitors strive toward a victory energizes me. In those moments I live vicariously through athletes and become completely caught up in the struggle. I love to see men and women pushing the edge, striving to reach the limits of human potential—it encourages me to dig down and find what I'm capable of. Very rarely will you find a man uninterested in some type of triumph.

For both men and women, discovering the adventurer within is invaluable as we seek to uncover and realize the reason for our being. If I pay attention to what captures my imagination, I can uncover important clues as I engage in the adventurous journey of learning and fulfilling my life's core ambition. One of my favorite ways to uncover these clues about my calling is through movies. The big screen has introduced me to passions and longings I didn't even realize I had. Rather than just walking away after an hour or two of entertainment, I try to take notice of what resonates in my heart and motivates me to be more of who I was designed to be.

When I saw *Braveheart*, I was transfixed by one man's absolute commitment to saving people from being murdered and oppressed. William Wallace was a man willing to risk everything for a cause worthy of his life. I'll never forget how deeply moved I was by his conviction, his devotion to truth and justice. I too desire to be a man who lives with bold courage. I want to be a man who loves with the fullness of passion, who wholeheartedly lives a rich and meaningful adventure. I am also aware of the many ways in which I'm not "all that." The point is, this is part of discovering the adventurer within me, finding desire to fully engage my life and grow into the fullness of all I can be. I *want* to be that kind of man. Seeing such passion and integrity motivates me toward finding that within myself, and thus more fully live.

The Notebook inspired a different part of my soul. This timeless love story of a couple walking together through daunting challenges is a tale within a tale of one man's devotion to his wife as she suffers from advanced Alzheimer's disease. His love for her is unshakable, most beautifully through the days and years of her not being able to remember who he is. Over and over he lovingly tells her the whole story of their life together, hoping through all the reminders that for a few fleeting, precious moments she will remember him. His adventure is to win his wife's heart again, every day. I want to be a man who loves that deeply, and with such complete loyalty.

On a much lighter note, I enjoyed the relational storyline in *The Mask of Zorro*. Elena, an impressive woman of conviction, gives Zorro a significant challenge by opposing him in an exciting sword fight. She more than holds her own with an in-your-face confidence; she's quite capable of taking care of herself. Still, she looks forward to taking refuge in the arms of a man who will protect her and fight for her honor. What inspires me is what Elena brings to them as a couple. Together, Zorro, the consummate old-world hero, and his new partner, who brings complementary strength and beauty, make an unbeatable duo committed to righting wrongs and bringing about justice. I want a *relationship* that embraces all life has to offer with a woman who's audacious, who's brave enough to join me in the adventure. Fortunately for me, I now have that!

Unrivaled is my hero and source of inspiration, the Lord Jesus Christ. I look to him as the model of how to live a life of courage and compassion. I know I will never be fully conformed to his image while here on this earth, but daily I want to discover more of what it means to be like Jesus, the world's greatest lover: undaunted in his passion, his courage, his devotion, his tenderness. His relationships changed the world forever. With the power of his Spirit, Jesus promised that together we can do even mightier things.

Many women are also driven toward adventure. After 9/11, my good friend and colleague Christine Arnzen was asked to intervene as a crisis worker at Ground Zero. In the midst of those uncertain days, she was excited by the opportunity to offer comfort to hurting families and first responders. Everything inside her urged her to accept, but other considerations caused her to hesitate. She had small children at home and a full-time job directing a university counseling center. Her absence even for two weeks seemed impossible. The restlessness began.

Christine has always been spurred on to do what she can to make a difference—large or small. Yet here she was caught in life's family chapter, and sometimes she felt as if she was just marking time. She rationalized that she was contributing to the future of her children, the students she counseled, and even the lives of her friends, but she wanted more. She wanted adventure.

The more she became aware of her yearning, the more she talked about it. Her friends encouraged her to go for it. But when she tried to discuss it with her husband, Jim, he would politely smile or just give her a blank look (or so it felt). She figured he didn't understand because he's analytical and steady, maybe not the kind to take risks.

The topic began to permeate most of her conversations, and at one point she thought her discontent was an indicator that she needed to pursue her doctorate. She decided against doing so, but one night during that time of searching she and Jim went for a walk. She again brought up her restlessness and her desire to stretch her wings. Again, Jim was silent.

They walked on for some time until Jim asked a question that caught her off guard and stopped her mid-stride: "Chris, when you say you want an adventure, do you see that as something to do by yourself, or do you see me in it with you?"

She stammered, "I'm not sure—why do you ask?"

He began to explain his concern about how her increased talk of adventure was implying she was discontent with him. If she wanted to venture forth as a personal experience, he told her he could understand but that in the end he'd feel left out. As he spoke, she heard feelings she didn't know he had: feelings that included love, respect, sadness, and resignation, to name a few, all existing in the midst of uncertainty and personal conflict.

He proceeded to tell her that he too longed to bring lasting impact and that raising their children was a big part of this for him. After losing his father at an early age, Jim had committed himself to meaningful involvement in his children's lives. He was determined to live a balanced life so he could make a difference— not to be pulled in by the many trappings of career and income.

More than anything, he wanted to experience fulfillment with Chris.

Their conversation turned to defining how they both could pursue adventure but still provide stability for their children. They even dreamed about what their goals would be when the children were grown. Less than a month later, I unexpectedly showed up at Chris's office to see if she'd be willing to consider working for me at the National Institute of Marriage. When she shared the opportunity with Jim, they both knew deep down that this was a new part of their calling, the adventure in which God had placed them.

Conclusion

Our marriage adventure becomes divinely inspired when we're able to recognize and embrace the significance of our journey together, empowered by the Holy Spirit. Being willing to submerge ourselves and encounter the obstacles, together overcoming the adversary in our quest—this is what it means to press on toward our "high calling" (Philippians 3:14). When we identify and embrace the importance of the cause we find ourselves fighting for, we begin to see the potential ways in which our efforts can have a lasting impact on the present and the future. Only then will we see *our love story* as a cause fully worthy of our whole hearts—worthy of living for and dying for.

Theodore Roosevelt once said, "Far better it is to dare mighty things, to win glorious triumphs even though checkered by failure, than to rank with those poor spirits who neither enjoy nor suffer much because they live in the gray twilight that knows neither victory nor defeat." Herein lies the first secret to *Finding Ever After:* When two lovers find themselves ready and willing, they engage in the adventure that is their own. Theirs is a *real* love story of epic proportions, husband and wife fulfilling their heart's truest desires by stepping into the leading roles of the life they were designed to live. We come alive when we discover that—together—our marriage relationship is an adventurous quest of eternal beauty and purpose.

─────────── *to* **P o n d e r** *and* **D i s c u s s** ───────────

1. Does your life seem meaningful? In what way?

2. How does your definition of adventure compare to the one used in this book?

3. In what ways are some of the more mundane parts of life potentially adventurous? Are there aspects of your life you now see as adventurous that you previously did not?

4. How closely aligned do you feel your life is to God's plan for your life?

5. What would fully embracing your "adventure" look like?

6. What changes would result if you embraced your "adventure" fully?

7. Think of your favorite characters from movies or books. Do they help you discover any clues about your calling and ambitions?

CHAPTER 3

— FASCINATED —
Discovering the Heart
of Romance

Where passion is not found, no virtue ever dwelt.
— Maria Brooks

Did you know the average woman would rather engage in an exciting romance than have all the riches in the world? Is it a surprise the average man would rather have an intimate romance than a series of hot one-night stands? None of us can say, "He (or she) is just not romantic." Why? Woven within the very fabric of our being is a yearning to transcend our separateness and connect deeply. That mysterious, enticing pull within each of our souls is what moves us toward one another.

Each of us, you say? If passion and romance are within every person, how can it be that many people are apathetic and impassive? The answer lies in how much people reveal and how deeply into them we see. Many *do* seem to be without passion and aspiration, but no one is summed up by what's on his or her surface. Whether the thickness of that surface is a millimeter or a mile, no matter the person, underneath it is an ocean of longing and desire.

What Were We Thinking?!?

My husband is *not* romantic. I don't think he's even capable of romance.

Ha! You want to know the last time we were romantic?!

Our romance is dead.

What comes to mind when you hear the word *romance*? For many of us, our thoughts wander back to magical preludes of infatuation. Most of us also remember budding romance that failed and likely resulted in hurt and disillusionment. With the past track records many of us share, romance can seem hopelessly complicated, practically unattainable, and even too dangerous to be worthwhile.

Have you come to believe that a marriage filled with excitement and passion is a fantasy fit only for a good movie? Shrouded in myth and far too often packaged with infidelity, romance has taken a bad rap. For many men, intimacy evokes disinterest or feelings of frustration and inadequacy; for many women, it stirs hopeful anticipation. We all may secretly wish for romance, but few are willing to ask for more—out loud, anyway. Life is lonely and painful when the warmth of intrigue cools and even freezes. As devastating as it is to lose our sense of adventure, we ache at the loss of wonder— the romance—that draws us toward another human being.

Just as with adventure, we have a built-in need for romance to be all it's intended to be. The good news is, you'll soon discover that yours is *not* history. Your love life can still be all you long for it to be. You were designed to have your deepest longings met, and this is not as difficult or as complicated as we've been led to believe.

Some women enjoy being single, but not Lindsey. She never planned to remain unmarried until age twenty-eight, and she was beginning to give up all hope of romance being in the cards. She knew what she wanted in a husband, but her prince seemed nowhere to be found.

Lindsey's lover-less life didn't make any sense. She was outgoing and pretty and had a dynamic career. Men should be lining up, right? Chloe and Elaine, her best friends, sure thought so. They decided to take matters into their own hands, thinking maybe there was something to the old tradition of matchmaking. They would find the ideal man, then put him and Lindsey in a setting where they'd both be swept off their feet. Several weeks of intense planning yielded what appeared to be the mother lode of all romantic evenings. Complete with bachelor, it looked fail-proof.

Chloe's cousin, Brett, seemed to be Lindsey's ideal fit, and, much to the girls' delight, both Lindsey and Brett were willing participants. The two strangers were sent to a famed restaurant on the shoreline called Montego Bay. Every detail was sublime: exquisite cuisine, white sand beaches, candlelight, even a magnificent sunset. The seagulls and sounds of the surf added a musical touch. Lindsey and Brett were stunned at the care and preparation invested in this special night. Each secretly hoped this would be the first evening of an ongoing liaison.

Two beautiful people with interesting backgrounds and amiable personalities . . . one would think they'd have endless things to talk about and enjoy together. Instead, their dialogue began to feel like an interview. Brett thought Lindsey was attractive but he felt awkward, not wanting to blow it. Lindsey was worried that she wasn't what Brett wanted; she felt dull, and he looked restless. They were sitting close, sharing a gourmet meal against a backdrop of Caribbean sights and rhythms, and still they could hardly keep a conversation going. Everything was present but the spark of romance. Lindsey and Brett just didn't connect.

Lindsey returned home feeling depressed and bewildered. Throughout the next several weeks she reviewed the dismal scenario from every possible angle. Had her expectations been too high? When he never called again, her self-esteem took a plunge.

One night, needing to get out of her head as well as her apartment, she decided to make a late run to the only place still open, Wal-Mart; she would pick up necessities and pass the time until she felt tired enough to sleep. As she strolled through the aisles, her eye caught a travel book on the Caribbean, displaying a man and a woman locked in an embrace against a background of azure blues and palm trees. Feeling mocked and resentful, she wondered how she'd missed her chance at love in such a perfect setting. Her eyes brimming with tears, she aimed her cart toward the checkout. On autopilot, she paid and rushed from the store.

The night was cold, and rain had begun to fall. *How's this for being about as far from paradise as you can get?* Clenching her teeth, she sloshed her cart through the dark puddles and jammed her key into the car door. Too late she realized she'd wedged in the wrong key. Moments from a screaming fit, she began struggling to pull it out.

"Hey there, need some help?" Drenched, furious, and startled, she looked up and saw Luke, a friend of a friend she'd met several years back. She was embarrassed but relieved. "I seem to be stuck."

Luke grinned, and the awkward tension lessened. While he jimmied the key out of its tight fit, Lindsey tried to remember how she knew him. Just in time, she placed him—they'd been acquainted through mutual friends in college. She'd thought he was nice; she'd just never gotten to know him.

He helped load her bags into the car, and when a tub of Ben and Jerry's escaped and rolled across the trunk, he asked if she needed help with that too. With a smile she said that yes, perhaps she did. Their bodies were close, and she was taken with the way he looked into her eyes yet showed respect for her space. He seemed to care about how she'd been doing, and before long they were lost in conversation. He was genuinely interested . . . and interesting. How had she missed him before? While they stood there in the drizzle, Lindsey forgot about her soggy hair and lonely heart. The longer they talked, the more she saw tenderness mixed with a contagious playfulness. She definitely wanted to know more.

It was magical. *So this is why young lovers speak in cliché!* she thought. Luke asked if she'd like some coffee with the ice cream; Lindsey said she'd be happy to join him at Starbucks down the street. As she watched him splash through the rain to his truck, she laughed at the absurdity of it all—here in the middle of a Wal-Mart parking lot, on a cold, miserable night, her heart had been captured.

Enchantment in life can never be realized in some thing;
it must ultimately culminate in a person.
—Ravi Zacharias

How many of us think romance is *created* with things like cards, gifts, or flowers? Thanks to a steady media diet—shows, books, films, magazines, songs, and so on—we've come to believe romance spontaneously happens if we can get the *details* just right. We go to great lengths and spare no expense attempting to recreate emotions we once had, hopeful the amorous feelings might re-ignite. Sometimes we're fortunate enough to be enrapt for a moment or two, but invariably the feeling disappears. The truth is, none of these things actually "creates" romance.

You can put two people in the perfect setting with extravagant props and elaborate accessories, but *if they're not interested in each other, passion will never happen.* The essence of true romance is fascination with the other person. All the other details merely set the stage to enhance the experience of discovery. We cannot create romance; instead *we are created for romance . . .* and we are captured by it.

Curiosity: Created for Romance

Imagine with me the front pages of Creation. God waits with bated breath while Adam—awestruck—sees his bride for the very first time. I can be entertained for hours while wondering what those first days must have entailed. I envision God saying, "Come with me, son. Do I have something to show you! Any idea? Go ahead, take a guess." You see, the Master Artist carefully fashioned man and woman to have curiosity, wonder, and awe. Adam and Eve had enormous ability to learn and grow and to enjoy the journey of discovery. After all, they had a whole world and each other to learn about.

We also have been created *naturally curious,* with an amazing capacity to learn and grow. It's in our very DNA—we too have been given each other and a world to explore. We see this natural instinct while watching children. Watching my four kids crack the code to their world has been a favorite part of fatherhood for me.

When our eldest son, Chris, was a little tyke, he was into everything: looking, touching, tasting, climbing, anything he could get his hands on. One day he crawled over to a bookshelf in our living room and pulled himself up to a standing position. He then grabbed a large potted plant and pulled it down. By the time Jenni and I arrived a few seconds later, we found a pile of dirt in the shape of our little boy. Chris looked up at us with a big muddy smile of utter delight and satisfaction as if to say, "Wow! Isn't this neat?"

Whether it's a bug, a booger, or a new tune on the piano, when a child is given a safe and stimulating environment, he or she needs only a nudge of encouragement to continue pioneering through uncharted territory. At first everything is fascinating. Each new discovery is a delight that compels more curiosity. In a word, a child is *infatuated*, taken with an irrational passion "to know."

It is with this same feeling of intrigue that we find exhilaration in romance, making us come alive in life and with each other. Our curiosity propels us toward exploration. Exploration leads to discovery. Every new discovery delights, satisfies, and then prompts us toward more curiosity and exploration. Before we know it, we've become fascinated. This is the heart of romance—the spark that ignites the flame of passion and the fuel that keeps it burning.

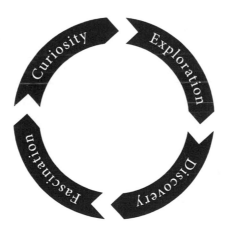

In his book *Recapture the Wonder*, Ravi Zacharias reveals that our heart's ultimate fulfillment is found in rediscovering and developing our God-given sense of wonder.

Deep within all of us is a longing to recapture a sense of

wonder, to marvel at the mystery of God and His creation like we did as children. But through the years our
capacity for wonder has been stifled by busyness and
ambitions, and we have resigned ourselves to explaining
away all that once made us gasp in awe. After all, how
can we let our hearts believe what our minds tell us is
nothing more than childish fantasy?[1]

"Unless you change and become like little children, you will
never enter the kingdom of heaven," Jesus said (Matthew 18:3).
Those who, like children, remain teachable and open to change
stand in stark contrast to the rest of us adults who quickly become
strangers to surprise. "Though maturity is good and necessary,"
writes Bill Ewing in *Rest Assured*,

> with it we lose the childlike freedom of our hearts and
> we take on adult hearts. . . . Why did God tell us to have
> a child's heart? He knew we'd never be able to fully know
> Him and each other unless our hearts remain open,
> inquisitive, and teachable without preconceived judg-
> ments, because without the journey of discovery to sat-
> isfy and captivate us we lose our motivation.[2]

The day we stop learning and growing together is the day marriage
becomes a holding pattern. When we cease to live in wonder, we
acquiesce to a standard of living that centers around feeling as
much pleasure and as little pain as possible—*surviving* until we die.

When Curiosity Sleeps

*I think, at a child's birth, if a mother could ask
a fairy godmother to endow it with the most useful gift,
that gift should be curiosity.*
—Eleanor Roosevelt

One of the most tragic stories I know involved a gentleman who
one day walked into my office. He'd had an affair and now in its

aftermath was filled with remorse. He knew he'd messed up and was genuinely pained by his failure's effect on his wife and kids, not to mention on his relationship with God. The romance in his marriage appeared to be completely dead. He never doubted he was married to a wonderful, caring woman; he'd been swept up in the affair as a result of longing to feel *alive* again.

"Bob, help us rekindle the flame," he pleaded, his eyes filling with tears.

When I began sharing about reclaiming fascination, however, his demeanor completely changed. He crossed his arms, and his face took on a hard expression. "I don't buy it," he said flatly. "My wife is a beautiful, loving woman, but she's just not that complicated. There's nothing about her I don't already know."

He was dead serious. "In fact," he said a bit more loudly, "I'd go so far as to challenge you, Bob, to come up with one thing I don't already know about my wife. I guarantee there is nothing."

I sat there stunned. When I finally found words, I said, "My friend, I hate to tell you this, but if that's your attitude, you're sunk; there is nothing I can do. Fortunately, I also know you're wrong." I then explained why.

Days later I saw that a meeting with his wife, whom I had yet to meet, was penciled in. When her appointment time came, into my office walked an attractive woman. Because of the boring portrait her husband had painted, I was surprised by how petite and stylish she was. Twisting her tissue, she proceeded to spill the contents of her heart.

"We moved to Southern California just months after our wedding." She shook her head. "I had no idea what lay ahead, but I immediately felt the pressure to hold my husband's attention over all the other stunning women in Orange County. Not only did I have to compete with the female co-workers at his office, he was a university student surrounded with hundreds of intelligent women.

I'm not sure how, but I developed this belief that I had to be fascinating to him . . . more so than all the female competitors who were in his classes, at the gym, on the beach . . . wherever.

"Little did I know what a losing proposition it was. How could I possibly hold Jack's attention? I'm simple and uninteresting. . . ." She began to sob openly. "I love him, but I'm hopeless. I've done everything I know to do. Now I know there's . . . nothing."

I could envision how exhausting and futile her marriage must have felt, and I told her so. She'd done everything she could to make herself interesting and attractive, and he had an affair anyway! My response went something like this: "I'm sure this all seems impossible, but Shari, I've got news for you. Jack didn't lose interest in you because you weren't interesting. You don't have to make yourself fascinating, because you already are."

At this she looked up in disbelief. I continued. "God created you with more than enough to keep any man who is willing to want to know you *fascinated for a lifetime.* You don't have to do anything. Your feelings, your dreams, what you're learning, all that God is doing with you and in you, is plenty to keep a man interested . . . if he is willing to stay curious and keep his heart open. If he allows himself to turn off his interest, it's his choice and his responsibility."

I knew there was plenty this man still didn't know about his wife, no matter how uncomplicated she may have seemed. An entire lifetime isn't nearly enough time to fully know *any* human being—yourself included. The Great Deceiver would love for us to believe that, contrary to God's inspired plan for lifelong intrigue and enthusiasm, love can sputter and die. When we fall prey to the lie that there's nothing left to discover about our spouse, the only way to feel alive is to search for intrigue outside the marriage. The truth is, marriage provides the *ideal* opportunity for the ultimate romantic experience. No other relationship is more perfectly designed for the lifelong interplay between exploration and being discovered—"knowing" and "being known."

Myth Dispelled, Truth Affirmed

I hold tightly to my choice to remain fascinated because I too had bought into a deadly falsehood that used to terrify me.

Myth: Romance and passion naturally fade over a lifetime.

I have a huge aversion to boredom and want nothing to do with it. I've seen far too many people apathetic with life and marriage. Whether they've been together a short time or for fifty years, they look like living dead people. Their lives are without spark, depleted of fascination and intrigue. I can't tell you what a breakthrough it was to learn the truth: *Passion only fades when people lose their curiosity.* When I realized God's intention was for me to live life in awe of him and my wife, I knew I'd never become lethargic in marriage because I choose otherwise. I'm always learning new things about Jenni. And just to keep things interesting, she keeps changing!

It's natural to have curiosity, yet we must determine to pursue it in order to retain a spirit of fascination; it's within our control. Some people think boredom comes and goes like a bout with the flu. However, *boredom never just happens; it is 100 percent man-made.*

Nothing about life is inherently dull. Did you know that we're responsible for our own apathy? When we feel bored, it's because we've lost touch with our imagination and shut down our inquisitiveness. Life becomes such a tedious routine when we reach a place of thinking we know it all and have seen it all. What an illusion. What a lie.

One of our society's core values is prizing newness and variety. In relationships, we're invariably set up for failure if we buy into the notion that unless we own the latest, sleekest young beauty, we're doomed to the doldrums.

Through more than a quarter century of marriage, I've been together sexually with my wife too many times to count. She continues to be stunningly beautiful to me, even after we've explored each other's bodies from head to toe. The only new *physical* discoveries we've yet to make have to do with watching the effects of gravity over time! I used to wear a baseball uniform at our conference on marital teamwork; my intention was to look like a player. But one day I looked in the mirror and noticed that my midsection was making me look more like a manager. I don't wear the uniform anymore. If we allow ourselves to believe we must find our sexual excitement in physical newness, the only answer *is* finding someone new.

There's no question that the initial stages of a romantic relationship are some of life's most exciting moments. Feelings of euphoria can be addicting, and we can easily develop expectations that those same emotions will be sustained forever. When those fireworks level off, couples often fall into the traps of (1) accepting disillusion and disappointment, thereby learning to settle for less, or (2) becoming consumed with restlessness and discontentment, then leaving the relationship in hopes of recapturing the thrill.

Truth: You have the power to assure endless years of romance.

Here's the good part of the story: Feelings of being fully alive and in love absolutely *should* be addicting. When I recognize every day that I have new things to discover about my wife, we come back together again—same bodies, but with new vigor and enthusiasm. When we do, we gain new understanding about each other, ourselves, and our relationship together. We are drawn close with new victories to share, and we wonder at the accomplishments God is constantly bringing to pass. By choosing to stay engaged and ready to learn, we're choosing to keep our intimacy fresh and alive. I'm a passionate man, and I want the flame of romance to burn brightly for the rest of my life. Needless to say, I will do everything in my power to see that it does.

Building a marriage that creates warmth both Jenni and I can enjoy takes time, preparation, and attention to detail. I want her heart continually attended to and cared for. I want to be her romantic hero, so I need to know her likes and dislikes, her needs and desires, her preferences and favorites. Steak or seafood? The beach or the mountains? Rock climbing or tanning by the pool? Since romance is ultimately a matter of the heart, I want my wife to know that her feelings are valuable and precious to me.

With what I've learned about her I can intentionally help foster an environment that expresses my love through attention to detail. In so doing, I warm her heart and assure my success. I have now spent years earning my PhD in Jenni Paul, and I will continue taking classes. And every bit of what I've just shared, she can likewise do toward me.

Don't forget, though, that details will not originate or create romance. *Attention to detail augments and accentuates the romance you already have.* The reason details matter *after* the romance already exists is that the details themselves aren't the point; they're not independent but are specifically tied to that one person, specifically designed for him or her.

Finding a Romantic Ever After

The most beautiful thing we can experience is the mysterious. It is the source of all true art and science. He to whom the emotion is a stranger, who can no longer stand in wonder and rapt in awe, is as good as dead.
—Albert Einstein

The lure of romance stems from the place inside us that asks, "*Can I have my chocolate cake and eat it too?*" Enticed by moments of connected, inspired vitality, we wonder: Dare we ask for more? We want to believe these encounters are more than fleeting pleasures reserved for dating and the honeymoon. How do we live so that the mundane blends with the dramatic, so that the whole story of our marriage remains sensational? Here is Donna's story:

> During the years I attended university and graduate school, I lived at breakneck speed, working forty hours a week and taking a full course-load. I enjoyed the competition and fought hard for the highest scores and top positions. Crunching data, studying long into the night, I thought I had life by the tail. What I didn't realize was how clueless I'd become to the profound beauty of the area in which I lived and the people with whom I was sharing life, including my husband and kids. I was pushing hard to meet deadlines and to do research that was literally draining the life out of me.
>
> An extreme decision to move twelve hundred miles away from our life in the metropolis to a little ski town nestled in the Rocky Mountains was the beginning of a remarkable journey. With the drama of wide-open spaces and spectacular simplicity, our days played out like a movie from generations past. Though not at all a logical or practical move, I quickly found myself lost in love . . . not yet with another person or location, but with the discovery of my own heart.
>
> I've learned that I am a romantic through and through—in fact, I'm now realizing just how integral it is to my design. Yet I thrive on adventure too. Part of the romance of this "crazy" move to the great outdoors was the risk of venturing into the unknown. I had embarked on a journey both outward and inward. Life was full of literal dangers and perils. My family and I had to learn

to survive—make fire, gather food, etc.—and I had no choice but to listen to my deepest fears and joys with all my senses.

I first discovered my newfound passion for life by spending quiet time alone. And I had a lot of it. It was a profound gift God gave while bringing me through a severe illness that forced all my driven endeavors to come grinding to a halt. All my interruptions were gone. We had no phone, Internet, television, freeways. I had no job or business meetings, and no local friends yet. At last I had time and attention to acknowledge the grace and beauty surrounding me. I could see how extravagant is God's care for detail.

Romance is now a gift I share with myself, my Lord, *and my lover.* I have learned to slow down, to quit striving, and to be more gentle with others and myself. I worship more readily in the quiet. Especially while writing, I treat myself to a romantic setting. A gorgeous view outside my window beckons me to come outdoors each day. I have inspiring art on the wall painted with warm colors. I surround myself with comfy furniture and fabrics that I love. I splurge with details that appeal to each one of my senses. Right now I'm sipping a hot drink; quiet music fills the background, and a fire crackles in the fireplace.

I want to live a life of wonder and awe . . . and I desire nothing more than to share it with the man I love the most. Together we are learning that romance is found in expectation, breathless anticipation of what's coming, the tantalizing unwrapping of an exquisite gift. It's an appreciation for simplicity, the attention to and care for detail. It is delicious flavors exploding in our mouths, texture, and poetry set to music. It's grace for the journey. Sensual. A romantic life for us means living a life of worship and deep gratitude whether we're together or alone.

Fascinating the Romantic

Romance is a universal longing, never determined by a place but always by an attitude; being fully alive without the push to be someplace else. It requires little movement. It's not about the future or about accomplishment but about being and resting in the moment, awake and connected to all that surrounds us. Romance is taking in the finest points of what we already have . . . with new eyes. These "grace notes" to life are often impractical and delicate—they can be easily steamrolled by daily routine.

For Her

While the inborn desire for romance is in us all, male and female, it's especially compelling for women. As the reflection of God himself, we are relational beings by design; in women this aspect of our nature is more developed, and, thus, typically feels more natural and essential. Romance is the primary doorway through which women enter the intimate world of marriage.

You may have wondered why women are generally more inclined to seek deep, lasting emotional connections. Outside of meaningful relationships, life (and career) quickly loses focus for most women. Much of a woman's intrigue is first found while unlocking clues to the mystery of lasting friendships. Her vitality surrounds and is profoundly connected to more deeply knowing others and being known; this is what I call *the inward journey, or the journey of the heart.* To a woman this feels like the core of life; it's central to feeling fully alive.

She loves things of beauty and longs to discover and express the beauty within her. She is drawn to the elegant dance of romance, and as part of that graceful movement she longs to delve into the depths of knowing her husband. Those more oriented toward relationship acknowledge and especially appreciate their spouse's devotion to them and their family. A partner's dedication to work, to the church, or whatever one's cause may be, is important, but without a healthy romance one's endeavors will feel lost on the romantic— as if life is happening all around her but not *with* her.

For Him

"Chels, what's the matter?" Rodney came up and wrapped his arms around his wife's shoulders, tightly enveloping her tiny frame with a hug. She stiffened.

Chelsea was being moody again. If this was another one of those hormonal things, he was going to be bummed. He was powerless over such things, and he knew better than to ask. Trying to choose his words carefully he said, "Honey, what *is* it?" He slipped his hand around her waist, inching it upward ever so slightly while gently pulling her toward him.

With a huff, she pushed away.

Shoot, wrong maneuver.

Chelsea had seemed delighted with his renewed sense of mission following their marriage intensive at NIM. In the past several months, Rodney had made great strides. He felt like God had breathed new life into his lungs, and he was inhaling deeply.

"Rodney, you just don't get it."

You got that right. "Try me," he said, trying to sound patient while reaching for a dish towel. He loved his wife more than life itself, but he had no idea what else he could do or be for her that he wasn't already. She used to complain that he wasn't taking his share of responsibility and that his life was void of passion. But he'd changed all that. They'd even been going out on dates a couple of times a month. Their lovemaking had been good, although he could always do with a little more each week. Now met again with Chelsea's rumblings of discontent, he wondered if he'd ever win.

Defeat is never pretty, and men love to win—we're just not always sure what victory is or how it looks when it comes to romancing our wives. The good news? It doesn't have to be a losing deal. As we saw in chapter 2, most men are willing to sacrifice their life for a cause worth dying for, but they need to be able to clearly see the purpose. Similar to his craving for adventure (the outward journey) and his need for understanding his calling, a man will ask of intimacy (the inward journey), "What's the point?" Far too often we're left feeling clueless or hopeless, feeling that no matter what, we cannot make the grade relationally. Wives, listen carefully: Nothing deflates a man more quickly than feeling incompetent. Men are drawn to romance but often shy away for fear of not knowing how to be successful.

For him, intimate relationships can seem nearly impossible to unravel, and he can't tell if he's winning or losing. If he doesn't already know his purpose, his cause will rarely include or justify the risk of a weeping or angry woman! Unless he can find a compelling reason, worthy of the risk, he'll most often choose to tiptoe carefully through the house on his way to making connections that don't seem nearly as dangerous (like a game of hoops). Ultimately, if he isn't empowered in romance, a husband will surrender the dream of finding an inward Ever After with his wife.

Most men want to make a meaningful difference. They strive to be impressive and inspiring to those who know and rely on them. As such, it's much easier for a man to do loving things for his wife than to relate intimately. Like Rodney, when he cautiously approaches, he receives what appear to be mixed signals, ones he doesn't know how to decode. Without guidance toward passion and an understanding of his true desires, he might eventually give up on the idea of being able to successfully romance her.

Here's the bright side: Rodney—in fact, every man—only needs two keys to enter into the romantic realm:

(1) He needs a clear comprehension of why he would risk venturing into and remaining in the dangerous territory of romantic love. He needs to know that what will be accomplished is of great enough significance to risk all the uncertainty. Give a man a clear picture of a noble, meaningful cause, and he'll be far more willing to take the risk or make the sacrifice.

(2) He wants to be trained and equipped to be successful in intimacy. Teach him how to win in life and how to be a hero in his home, and you will likely find him not only willingly but *enthusiastically* signing up! (In the coming chapters we'll provide tools for both.)

Conclusion

Romance. It's that mysterious force satisfying our inborn desire to transcend separateness, to connect deeply with what's closest to us. Once it's been ignited, all the trappings of romance fan the flame and stoke the fire. That romance sparked for Lindsey and Luke in a Wal-Mart parking lot by no means indicates that it's the ideal place to set up camp and build their campfire—for them or for anyone else. Location isn't the issue; without fascination the world's most amazing environments will not create romance. But when fascination is there first . . . watch out!

We saw in chapter 1 that *inspiration* is being fully alive from within, vitalized and ever revitalized by the life-giving breath of God. In chapter 2 we saw that *adventure* is the active pursuit of life, feeling the blood coursing through your limbs, readying for action and then taking it. Now we've seen that *romance* is the thrill of entering the sanctuary of another's embrace with a restful sigh.

Romance is being known and understood, being revered and adored, awakening each day with the expectation of new and exciting possibilities. The complementary, awe-filled experience of adventure and romance, shared between a man and a woman, summarizes for me what life is intended to be—the thrill of wonder and the irresistible urge to share it.

That's exactly what we want to do. Let's find out where. And how.

──────── *to* **Ponder** *and* **Discuss** ────────

1. When you hear the word *romance,* what comes to mind?

2. How has your definition of romance compared to the one used in this book?

3. What was it that so fully captured your attention, curiosity, and fascination about your spouse?

4. Is there something new you have recently discovered about yourself?

5. What are the potential benefits and risks of disclosing your passions, hopes, and dreams?

6. What is the difference between slowing down and boredom?

7. Does the idea of "choosing to be fascinated with your spouse for a lifetime" seem like something that would be difficult or relatively easy for you?

CHAPTER 4

—EMBRACE—
The Point of Contact

*When we are motivated by goals that have deep meaning,
by dreams that need completion, by pure love that needs
expressing—then we truly live life.*

—Greg Anderson

Friday night. All the kids were out. My wife and I had the evening to ourselves. "Hey Jen, what do you say we kick back tonight and watch a movie?"

We're just now getting glimpses of an empty nest, and Jenni gave me that look I wish I could see more often. "I thought you'd want to go out, but my week has been crazy," she said. "I'd love to spend some quiet time together."

"What should we watch?" I asked, thinking that deferring to her preferences would show her how much I love her . . . and score a few points.

She paused and narrowed her eyes a little while she thought. Then her face lit up and her eyes opened wide as if a prize package she'd been expecting for weeks had suddenly arrived. "You know what I've wanted to watch again?"

"No. What?"

"*Sense and Sensibility!*" Her enthusiasm could hardly be contained. After all, this is one of her all-time favorites.

I don't know if words can adequately capture how far my heart sank, knowing I'd done this to myself. *That will teach me to put her first.* I mean, honestly, I was okay the first time we saw it. I even somewhat enjoyed it despite the interminably slow pace and the sheer volume of melodramatic dialogue. But a second time? Jenni's seen *Sense and Sensibility* over and over and never seems to tire of it; I think I'd have more fun plucking out my eyebrows.

I was wanting something with a little more *action* and a little less *drama*. In a matter of thirty seconds I went from feeling brilliant in my wife's eyes to feeling like an idiot facing a self-made dilemma. Should I sacrifice my enjoyment to be her knight in shining armor, or should I surrender and be true to myself by sharing how badly I don't want to watch that movie?

You may not run into such scenarios with your spouse, but this is a common one. When it comes to movies, guys are often drawn in by high technology, warehouses full of weapons, a few chase scenes, and plenty of explosions thrown in for good measure. We thrive on suspense as we watch men of valor bleeding for country, family, and lover. Film doesn't get any better than when, against insane odds, the protagonist digs down to find enough spirit and courage to stomp the enemy. This leaves the average guy feeling pumped up and satisfied.

In contrast, most women prefer *Return to Me* over *Rambo*. They pack theaters with the hunger to enter into the intricacies of human drama. Women like to be caught emotionally and be brought into the lives of the characters. For a woman, so much of life's meaning is found relationally; rich dialogue enables her to know these people and feel for them. It also allows her to witness the beauty of an unfolding love affair as two hearts connect in a crescendo of love and passion.

The stereotypes don't apply to everyone—there are men who prefer Hugh Grant and women who favor Vin Diesel—but they're common enough that I'm sure you can relate. These realities lead to enough frustrations in marriages that you've probably bumped into them at least occasionally, if not regularly. In this vein, Hollywood takes full advantage of human nature, exploiting its savvy in attracting people to the product. Standard guy movies and chick flicks are generally made profitable by following a predictable formula.

When producers want to invest in a real blockbuster, however, they follow a different formula altogether. To create a film for the masses, a box-office bombshell, filmmakers must portray a gripping adventure that imbeds a captivating romance. For the average man, enough intense action allows him to thoroughly enjoy the romance. For the average woman, enough romance and passion in the adventure enhances the love story. Everybody loves the experience and can't wait to tell their friends.

The movie moguls have done nothing more than uncover a truth that already exists within the basic makeup of men and women. *The formula for an Oscar-award-winning marriage is the same.* A thrilling mission that includes an intimate liaison between two lovers appeals to both men and women and more fully satisfies a deeper side of us all.

The Point of Contact

A blockbuster marriage, one you can fully enjoy and share with a person who at times seems to want the exact opposite of what you want, may be closer than you think. The solution is profoundly simple and elegant: We feel most complete when our life is in balance between the *outward* journey and the *inward* journey—exciting adventure spurred on by impassioned romance. Though as males and females we tend to enter the relationship through opposite doors, and though, again, there are myriad gender differences, within each of us lives both an adventurer and a romantic. In our most basic essence we are not from different planets, we are all beloved children of God; part of the same body, members of the same spiritual family. We are designed to be fully capable of creating a dynamic, intimate marriage that thrills us, blesses the Lord, and inspires others.

For a man, the adventure alone is not enough to satisfy his soul because he was not meant to be alone. Pursuing a cause without someone to do it for and share it with is ultimately empty. From the doorway of adventure, a man can most easily engage and completely enjoy the intimate relational journey; only then does it become an *adventurous romance.*

For a woman, the romance alone is not enough to satisfy her soul because she was created with broader purpose. Romance opens the door to engaging the adventure. In many ways, the romantic journey *is* the adventure. For her, the journey can become a *romantic adventure.*

The ideal point of connection occurs when he can join her in the romance and she can join him in the adventure. Neither man nor woman needs to become like the other. They can each enter through his or her preferred door and have their initial drive toward fulfillment satisfied while embracing at the point of contact (adventure meeting romance). In so doing, each will have his and her heart's desires made complete.

Embracing Our Underdeveloped Side

The self-explorer, whether he wants to or not,
becomes the explorer of everything else.
—Elias Canetti

The first step in making your marriage a smash hit is yours—it begins with you. Since within each person is both a romantic and an adventurer, every one of us must embark on both the inward and outward journeys to experience life's fullness and to express all that God intended. If one side or the other is ignored or neglected, one can survive. But we know and have seen that survival is not the ultimate goal—there is far more to be attained.

It's likely that one side or the other of your orientation (adventurer/romantic) is underdeveloped, or at least less developed than the other; you must commit to growing and stretching within that less developed side. This does *not* have to be conquered prior to sharing a successful journey. Some of marriage's most amazing moments occur through sharing the trek toward growing and becoming more of who you were created to be.

Rounding Out the Adventurer

If you are a full-fledged adventurer with a clear sense of direction and purpose but you've not yet developed the romantic within, you are probably a "doer" and are able to get much accomplished. You most likely have great propensity for keeping your eyes focused on the destination. Developing your romantic side will require you to pause and reflect on the meaning and significance of what you are doing, and then to take time to enjoy the moment.

The activity of reflecting shifts your focus inward and allows you to get in touch with your heart as well as with those around you. You can then more thoroughly enjoy the sense of accomplishment when it's coupled with an appreciation of its value in the big picture. God himself did exactly this after creating the universe.

> God saw all that he had made, and it was very good. And there was evening, and there was morning—the sixth day. Thus the heavens and the earth were completed in all their vast array. By the seventh day God had finished the work he had been doing; so on the seventh day he rested from all his work. And God blessed the seventh day and made it holy, because on it he rested from all the work of creating that he had done. (Genesis 1:31– 2:3)

Developing the romantic side requires a willingness to allow your curiosity to grow, followed by steps toward exploring uncharted waters of thoughts and feelings within you, your spouse, and your relationship. Since any true romantic experience engages one's heart, the adventurer must intentionally allow his or her heart to be moved by the moment. This requires a pause, being still long enough to allow inward awareness and exploration to occur, and then recognizing and affirming its value. Any encounter with someone or something of great worth can, if allowed, create feelings of awe, gratitude, and passion. *This is what it means to be captured by the romance of the moment.* Your reflections and emotions become an important part of what you now have to offer.

Rounding Out the Romantic

If your predisposition is toward being a romantic, you naturally possess a fascination with people, beauty, and detail. You may have a closely knit social network and love to "get deep." This is an admirable gift; it means you're likely a "feeler," able to profoundly impact and affirm others through relationship.

Romantics in the extreme, however, can be so focused on what lies up close that they miss what's happening beyond the confines of their personal world. Developing your adventurer self will require looking out further to see how you can also make a difference beyond the scope of your personal relationships.

This necessitates asking God to begin revealing the full scope of your being—the "what" he has for you to do in this life—and then taking steps toward investing in activities that will accomplish that goal. As you begin to embrace your own calling toward the outward adventure, you move into being able to link arms with your spouse, like Christine did with Jim. She didn't have to strike out angrily on her own. As they communicated and worked together, she was able to explore her pull toward adventure and invite him to join her.

Since we all have been divinely created as both a romantic and an adventurer, very few people are so far to one extreme as to be completely undeveloped on their weaker side. We all have plenty of capacity with which to work. The key is recognizing the value found in tackling the investment in your own development and supporting your spouse in his or her own journey—this is embarking on your voyage together.

Cultural shifts over the last several decades have brought about monumental change in how we see our gender roles; some of these changes are helping to set the stage for what needs to occur in dynamic marriage relationships. Though many Christians have stood in broad opposition to social mores, I believe we can sift out the good as we hold up the whole spectrum to the light of God's truth. Throughout Scripture women are encouraged and given opportunity to engage in outward adventures. And, just as importantly, men throughout both Testaments are encouraged to engage with passion an inward romance on behalf of themselves and their people. At Pentecost, the boundary lines relating to worth and status were erased once and for all.

Until we get in touch with heart and soul, we cannot know the heart of God or see our own capability to powerfully impact the world for Christ. Men can still be real men of strength and conviction while also being relational, thoughtful in heart and soul. Women can still be real women of beauty and tenderness and yet be empowered with vision and boldness. At last, stereotypes are shifting and the door is being opened even wider for spiritual and relational transformation.

An Age-Old Legend, With a Spin

I just finished watching, for maybe the fourth time, a movie that has quickly become a favorite of mine. I can now keep company with preteen girls anywhere and even quote my favorite parts of the movie. Aside from everything little girls love about the enchanting tale, I cannot resist a story wherein a feisty maiden carries a prince out of the forest on her back. Independent, wise, inquisitive, resourceful, and compassionate, she's so much more complete than a distressed damsel. I let out a good hearty laugh when I realize she reminds me just a bit of my wife.

The film, coincidently titled *Ever After,* is based on the Cinderella story, but effectively challenges the happily-ever-after fantasy while reflecting a brilliant shift in the way women are portrayed. Unlike with the classic fairy tale, the leading character is Cinderella on steroids; she's driven by a purposeful sense of loyalty and righteousness. Fearless, she stands up for what's right, for the broader good, even when it's against the establishment. *Ever After* is not all about a floating maiden, an evasive prince, and a fantasy dance.

Drew Barrymore, cast as Danielle, the Cinderella character, is introduced as a child loved and valued by a father who helped her develop a passion for the outdoors, for reading, and learning. (Her mother had already died.) Now grown, she's smart, robust, and capable, with a healthy feminine side. In the years following her father's sudden death, following his marriage to her wicked stepmother, her focus has been fixed on the happenings of her immediate family, including two stepsisters, one of whom is boorish and evil and who joins her stepmother in making Danielle's existence miserable. Nevertheless, her education has created an awareness and ability to think and feel outside herself.

Through a remarkably entertaining series of events, Danielle unexpectedly attracts the attention of Prince Henry, and together they push past barriers limiting their acquaintance in a tightly castebound society. At one point, after they've wandered into the forest and gotten lost, Danielle removes her outer garment and climbs a tree to see if she can help navigate the way home. The prince, again impressed with the many facets of her personality, calls to the top of the tree, "You swim alone, climb rocks, and rescue servants; is there anything you don't do?"

"Fly," she says nonchalantly, and proceeds to climb back down.

Danielle captures viewers' hearts, both male and female, because she is "fully woman." On the one hand she's tomboyish, spunky, and unrelenting, while on the other she's charming, beautiful, and alluring. And so she captures Henry's heart. The prince has met his match, and, rather than being turned off or shut down, he's motivated and intrigued.

———————

Upon meeting Prince Henry, we also find the antithesis of a typical hero. Henry is dissatisfied with the world and the role he's being forced to play, especially concerning his upcoming arranged marriage and coronation. He doesn't realize he's looking for something more until he bumps into the lovely, loving-hearted commoner. A romantic collision with the resilient Danielle begins the adventure through which the prince will become all he was meant to be.

It is through his growing intrigue with this woman of conviction that Henry will find his own purpose and meaning. Danielle challenges the prince repeatedly to look deeply within and discover who he really is, who he was created to be, to connect his dreams with what he's been given to make a meaningful difference in the world.

As the accidental relationship begins to develop, Danielle continually questions Henry's seemingly shallow and arrogant approach to life. In one powerful scene he takes her to a library and discovers her undying love of books and learning. Amazed once more by her passion, in contrast to his own demeanor, he exclaims, "You have more conviction in one memory than I have in my entire being."

Later, after Henry has shared some of his frustration about his unwanted status in life, he laments, "I have no desire to be king." When Danielle responds, "Oh, but think of all the wonderful things you can do for your country, for the world!" he continues: *"Yes, but to be so defined by your position. To never be seen as 'who' you are, but 'what' you are. You have no idea how insufferable that is."*

The irony of that statement is central to the entire story. I love the way Danielle boisterously stimulates and exhorts Henry on both the *inward* romantic journey, to discover the unmet longings asleep within, and the *outward* adventurous journey, to become the fullest expression of who he can become. She dares him to engage completely the challenge of finding a meaningful cause, one worthy of investing his life.

Eventually the dividing obstacles are overcome; Henry and Danielle marry. Their real story, their together story, has yet to begin. *Ever After* is the backstory—what lies ahead for Prince Henry and Princess Danielle is the full embrace of their shared quest (given as a quick glimpse in the movie's epilogue). She had the more developed personality from the start, and because he's open to developing his weaker side, we're left without any doubt that this couple *will* find their Ever After in a future filled with happiness and gallantry—love and justice, passion and vision, romance and adventure.

Embracing in the Journey Together

The great renewal of the world will perhaps consist in this,
that man and maid ... will seek each other not as opposites,
but ... as neighbors, and will come together as human beings.
—Rainer Maria Rilke

Borrowing from the words of Rilke, let "the great renewal of the world" begin! When husband and wife are committed to embracing one another's journey, nothing can stand in their way—as long as they themselves don't stand in the way of God's blessings. Remember: God created our life through an act of inspiration, and he wants our life and relationships to remain fully alive and full of him. There is no greater draw to the kingdom of God than when followers of Christ, through his Spirit's work in both their inward and outward journeys, together display a love and vitality that others haven't yet found and still long for.

We noted in chapter 1 that people are giving up on marriage in record numbers. Many now question whether marriage can really work for the long haul in the contemporary world. However, if what Jesus said is true, marriages with him can and should look significantly different from marriages without him. I believe we *can* discover how to experience so much richness and fullness in a life with Christ that those around us will say, "Wow, that's what I want."

So get this! One of the all-time greatest ways to serve God is to help people find their own Ever After by learning to stay personally full, having an abiding relationship with the Lord and an awesome marriage with your spouse. When we capture a vision like that, we can see plainly how the challenging journey is worth the risk. The questions "Why bother?" and "What's the point?" no longer go unanswered. In the journey together, men and women can truly become heroes and heroines for the cause of Christ.

Living a fully inspired life requires our whole being to have opportunity to be grown, expressed, and experienced. Once again, I know of no other place more perfectly designed to discover and stretch one's complete potential than within the sanctuary of marriage. The next step, then, is to join and complement your spouse in the journey together—to embrace!

Every one of us has in himself a continent of undiscovered character. Happy is he who acts the Columbus to his soul.
—Sir J. Stevens

Embrace! When the Adventure Becomes an Adventurous Romance

Whereas both men and women can be adventurers by nature, men more readily approach life from this perspective; so looking at some common male traits can be helpful here. Many men most easily connect with others while rallying around a cause and working together. Men typically experience "being known" as the natural result of connecting with each other in battle, which could be anything from a real battle to the workplace to the golf course. In the throes of combat and competition we see what each other is made of—in other words, how much heart the other has. With adventure, victory is found while accomplishing a task of marked significance. Success achieved through stretching our limits leads to tremendous satisfaction and celebration. Guys love to sit back and admire one another's accomplishments, and we relish having others admire ours, at least by swapping a war story or two.

We are told that to be a real man one must be able to demonstrate cunning and skill in most "manly" areas of life. That status is commonly "granted" through various types of initiation rights and through comparisons to other men. To affirm valor, men often prove manliness with strength, courage, winning, overcoming fear and obstacles, being in control, status, achieving success with women, etc.

In stark contrast, the world of romance appears layered with emotional obstacles we're not sure we can overcome: desires, disappointments, phobias, passions, and so forth. We have a tendency to pay closest attention to the needs and wishes we're most familiar with while staying furthest away from those that pull us away from comfort. One realm in which men often feel least capable is that of romance and intimacy (the journey inward). Intimacy is the art of connecting heart to heart, of knowing and being known. This requires a man to put down his sword and shield, remove his armor, and allow the whole truth of who he is to be revealed, including his weaknesses and imperfections. These are likewise the very elements that challenge his ability to be confident about having what it takes to belong to and be successful in the world of men.

As John Eldredge showed in *Wild at Heart,* the basic question the average man feels compelled to answer is, "Do I have what it takes" ... to be successful, powerful, and inspiring in this world?[1] We spend an inordinate amount of time and energy on our response, and how we respond deeply impacts how we approach life and relationships.

Many men feel they don't quite measure up to the mark of being a "real man." And yet all men have been endowed by God with emotions and soft spots. Men are wrongly taught that they must conceal or ignore these; that if they don't, at the least they'll appear weak, at worst they'll be exposed as an utter fraud, and either way they'll be less of a man. In reality, it takes tremendous strength and courage to deal honestly and effectively with the more vulnerable and tender sides of life. The inward journey of the heart, every bit as adventurous as any outward pursuit, involves a quest to understand more fully who we are, what we're capable of becoming. Created for romance, a man can become free to relax in the arms of his trusted lover, knowing he is accepted and respected. Only *after* dropping his armor with his wife can a husband be confident in himself as a man and know that he is her romantic hero.

Another major challenge for men is either being unwilling or unskilled in making room for his wife to have a significant role in the inspired adventure. The happily-ever-after fairy tale often portrays the independently powerful knight rescuing the obviously helpless damsel. So many men and women have tried to play out this storyline, with unfortunate and even devastating personal and relational consequences. Herein are two critical problems, both stemming from the reality of our humanity. To husbands:

First, the knight in shining armor is not portrayed as a real flesh-and-blood man who has real fears and weaknesses. You *are* a real human man, and a real-to-life relationship with a real live woman in a real-world adventurous love story requires you to live in a way that's consistent with the truth about who you really are, not a false fantasy of who you allegedly should be.

Second, your wife deeply desires to be loved, cherished, and protected ... yet she was created by God as a strong, capable woman of purpose. *Invite her to join you in the adventure as your trusted partner.* Your roles may be different, but the cause is the same. Now you will not only be engaged in a worthy quest, you will also be cultivating a dynamic, meaningful union with a woman who's at the heart of your purpose. Your energy is not only invested in the cause but also in the relationship.

When a man allows himself not only to fight, provide, and protect, not only focusing outward to the job at hand but also turning inward to connect with and know those inside his castle gates, he moves to another level of relating. A romantic hero is one who also allows himself to be motivated and intrigued by the unique beauty and value of his most intimate relationship. When he is willing to join together with his wife as partners in the adventure, he has fully engaged the adventurous romance.

Embrace! When the Romance Becomes a Romantic Adventure

The warm exchange of the romantic journey tends to encourage people to open their hearts and keep them open; this makes a deep emotional connection possible. Women are frequently more comfortable than men in the romantic realm and are generally willing and able to enter into intimacy's risky areas as long as they feel moderately safe and secure. For a woman, the inward journey's excitement and value, through curiosity, exploration, discovery, and fascination, is often more easily understood and appreciated.

Though women are strong and adventurous in their own right,

many are still more inclined to focus inward toward the intricacies of relationship. We see this when a pregnant woman's natural focus turns inward toward the growing child while she prepares for its arrival. It often takes a conscious decision for a woman to turn her focus outward toward an even bigger purpose. This encouragement is in no way meant to minimize the incredibly important role she may play in nurturing and developing her family; what I mean to say is, this certainly is not all there is to her life and ultimate significance. Many women need to grow in willingness to see beyond the limits of how they have defined themselves and/or who they've felt they should be.

For romantics to connect with adventure, they first must be willing and able to recognize the importance and value of fully engaging the outward journey. This means being able to appreciate how much genuine passion arises in the midst of adventure. A woman is likely to feel that adventure for its own sake is a mere pushing of human limits just to see if something can be done. However, if the adventure is driven by deep passion for a human cause and includes the opportunity to strive together and share in the moment, she can easily get on board. The potential to learn and grow through outward exploration while sharing a life of significant purpose is extremely romantic. As long as the relationship remains the primary focus and the couple is able to connect deeply through the experience, it is a romantic adventure.

John and Stasi Eldredge beautifully capture the essence of the feminine quest in their book *Captivating*.[2] They suggest that deep inside a woman's heart resides a question about whether she is truly captivating, fascinating, and alluring. Will a man find her lovely and long to explore the depths of her being, motivated onward by the beauty he also discovers within? Women spend an enormous amount of time, energy, and money attempting to answer that question and become that woman. How they answer deeply impacts how they approach life and relationships. Many women struggle in the realm of adventure, some because they feel insecure and vulnerable and some because they feel unwanted and unwelcome.

A woman will always have an easier time recognizing her own innate strength, ability, and courage when she feels safe in her marriage and feels invited to the partnership of adventure. Even though more and more women today are discovering the awesome gifts God has placed within them, many hesitate to enter an adventure with their husband for fear of being unwanted. She feels far safer staying with the romance and avoiding the adventure, even if a part of her remains largely ignored.

Women *can* search within to find the place where God is inspiring them to employ unique gifts and become a part of a wondrous outward journey with their husbands. They may or may not feel any need to *lead* such an undertaking, though the Eldredges point out that women generally desire to "play an irreplaceable role in a great adventure." Unfortunately, many often feel left out; women regularly complain to me that their husband is looking for a playmate, not a partner. While playing together can be fun and rewarding, outward adventure alone won't satisfy a woman's desire to share with her mate in a meaningful enterprise.

Wives: One major challenge centers on what to do if you're ready and able to join with your husband on an outward journey but he isn't ready or doesn't know how to share it. I first want to encourage you to stay connected to God's purposes, becoming and being actively involved in a life of meaning and purpose by following wherever he leads you—home, church, work, and anywhere else. There are areas in which your choices and actions alone can make a tremendous difference.

Your sadness and loneliness may result from not yet being able to share this together. You may be living an adventure, but up to this point it isn't the romantic adventure you long for. *Patience is critical in praying and hoping for change.* Consider periodically expressing your disappointment with not being included in his adventure or with him not joining you in yours. Occasionally invite him to join you. Attempt to understand what is meaningful to him; discover where he wants to invest or is already investing himself, and continue to watch for opportunity. *God is not finished with him or with your marriage.* (We'll address dealing with disappointment and grief in chapter 9.)

To engage in the adventure you must be clear about what it is you're being called to do and why it's important—that is, what kind of impact it will have on the kingdom. Identifying and clarifying the cause means connecting with a vision you can be passionate about and share in together; a common cause you can embrace together that gives your life lasting meaning. As a result you'll naturally be engaged in a journey of learning more about yourself, your husband, life, relationships, and God, which will additionally pique your interests and satisfy your needs.

Putting It All Together:
An Extreme Example

I can't think of one person I know who's more committed to living a romantic adventure than my friend Gail. She and her husband, Jeff, have had a journey like few others. They've now been married twenty-five years, but about eighteen years into the journey Jeff's business was consuming him; his marriage and family were suffering from the busyness and nonstop stress. He felt an overwhelming need to get away to find his sanity and restore his life, faith, and family. He became captured by the notion of shutting down his business, selling everything, and buying a boat to sail the high seas with Gail and their three boys. What began as an outlandish fantasy to recapture life's fullness led him to wonder, "What if we could actually make it happen?"

His idea was met with wide-eyed disbelief when he presented it to his wife. "You can't be serious?!" was her first reply.

The thought of giving up their home, leaving friends and family, and stepping away from everything that represented stability and security sounded horrible to Gail. But Jeff was struggling under the weight of their life, and as a result so was the whole family. She agreed to pray about it, and with time and lots of prayer, she began to feel a divine peace. As she caught the vision she realized they "weren't going sailing to escape life; they were sailing so that life would not escape them." Much to her own surprise, in the end she agreed to go. She was willing to embark on an outward adventure with Jeff, driven by an inward desire to reconnect.

They sold everything, bought an old, bright-red, fifty-foot Gulfstar (named *Riverwind*), and set sail from Florida to traverse the Caribbean for eighteen months. Neither of them had any significant sailing experience, so this wild idea was either divinely inspired or just plain stupid. Their goal was to get "unhooked" from the ways of the world and "untangled" personally and relationally.

At times Gail was terrified, and many times she questioned her own sanity. The challenges were many, the stories outrageous. In the first week alone they saved two boats from sinking, ran *Riverwind* up on a reef in the southern Bahamas, went through a storm that ransacked both boat and crew, and one night were thirty seconds from being run over by an oil tanker. There were also unforgettable times of exploring uninhabited islands, encountering amazing sea life, home-schooling together, and making new friends from all over the world.

———

They came back forever changed. What they learned about each other, about life, and about God will one day make its way into a book of their own. But that's not the end of the story.

For six years now they've been back, reengaging the real world with all its daily challenges. Jeff has continued to find opportunities to invest what he's learned back into the world. He's involved in adventures of great meaning and purpose, giving his time and talent to help anyone he can. One of his passions is heading up an organization called the Marriage CoMission, designed to mobilize communities, marriage ministries, and businesses to cooperate in reversing negative trends in American families. Gail has kept her focus on raising their boys and maintaining the family, but she's always involved in other outwardly focused activities also, which includes helping Jeff with CoMission events.

Jeff and Gail as a couple are committed wholeheartedly to living as teammates in the great adventure of life. Gail is engaged in more fully discovering the multitude of gifts God has placed within her while finding new outlets to express them. Jeff is determined to learn how to continue making room for Gail to find her stride and not hinder her as she does. Their journey is far from complete, and there's plenty more to learn, with enormous challenges ahead. After all, theirs is *a real-life love story.*

Conclusion

We want to be empowered so that, like Jeff and Gail, we too might embrace one another—becoming active, interlocking players in the drama set before us. On occasion I'm even willing, like Gail, to venture into the dangerous unknown. Tonight that simply means tapping into my underdeveloped self and watching *Sense and Sensibility* one more time.

As I sit here on the couch, reveling in the romance of my marriage, my mind wanders while Edward and Elinor stroll the grounds of the estate. Her shawl slips off her shoulders; he gallantly swoops down, picks it up, and replaces it. The film's still not my favorite, but I can't help smiling as I'm reminded of my wife's integral role in our journey together—the power of how she fully engages in life and thereby inspires and draws out her counterpart into fullness. I reach for a tissue.

Ultimately, we know that true "happily ever after" comes not with perfect bliss but with the continued camaraderie of shared passion and vision. It isn't until we allow ourselves to be allies on an epic quest that we fully experience our real love story. If you want a blockbuster marriage, it's well within your reach! Part Two of *Finding Ever After* is about the practical steps to making the journey all you hope it can be.

--------- *to* Ponder *and* Discuss ---------

1. Using the definitions from this book, in what ways do you gravitate toward adventure and in what ways toward romance?

2. On a scale of 1–10 (10 being extreme), rate the extent to which you fully engage your life as an adventure, and then rate the extent to which you fully embrace romance in your life.

3. How do your perceptions of yourself compare to how your spouse sees you?

4. What do you see as the difference between an adventurous romance and a romantic adventure?

5. As a woman, what is it like to see a man being tender?

6. As a man, what is it like to be tender? How much strength and courage do you think it takes to exercise this part of you?

7. As a man, what is it like to see a woman be strong and act on conviction?

8. As a woman, what is it like to be strong and act on conviction? How much strength and courage do you think it takes to exercise this part of you?

Part **TWO**

CHAPTER 5

— ALLIES —
All for One and One for All

Success demands singleness of purpose.
—Vince Lombardi

We now have a map for finding our way to a place where two divergent paths meet, where husband and wife can connect and share a common journey. We may emphasize different aspects of the journey, but we know men and women both want and need adventure and romance to feel fully alive and satisfied. Even so, inevitably we won't go far before bumping into challenges that stem from our respective orientations toward life. We may find ourselves repeatedly at an impasse. We may find ourselves asking, "Why does opposition keep happening? Aren't we ever going to be past this?!" *Why is it that even after realizing they're headed in the same direction, couples still wrangle their way through marriage?*

Rare is the relational conflict that doesn't stem from an issue of gender or personality difference. Often considered the enemy of oneness and unity, though, the contrast between male and female perspective is meant to be *the* blessing and not a subject of dispute. Troubles arise not from dissimilar perspectives but from not knowing how to value and work with individual differences.

Let's examine some perceived obstacles to unity, the ones most likely to railroad couples into becoming adversaries instead of allies.

The No-Fighting Zone

Conflict is not only normal, it can also benefit both of you personally *and* benefit your marriage. First and foremost, however, I want you to know that I do not endorse *fighting of any kind*. You read that right. None. Not any. While many well-meaning marriage experts teach "fair fighting" rules, I'm not one of them. Marriage is ideally a no-fighting zone.

Despite the inevitability of *conflict,* there are plenty of ways to handle our disputes that do not require a *fight* and the far-reaching damage that follows in its wake. I realize this idea might be hard to swallow, and I promise I won't leave you hanging for long, but before we get to the solution I want to take a closer look at some of the complications of trying to live in peace and harmony.

We humans share many more things in common than we usually realize, yet we're wired so uniquely that we approach situations from a broad span of views. Our diverse ideas, backgrounds, and experiences bring with them a whole continuum of expectations; because we all have different beliefs and feelings, we all have distinct preferences. If you haven't encountered this with your spouse, you're either in a coma or blinded silly by young love. Throw in a dash of this and add a little of that to two heaping cups of built-in gender differences and watch the mix come to a rolling boil! How many of your quarrels didn't result from dissimilar points of view?

We naturally assume that *differences* are the enemy and that we need to get rid of them.

As a way of trying to anticipate and avoid future discord, many of us determine that the goal in looking for a spouse is to find someone with whom we have the most in common—finding a package deal with the fewest possible differences. We surmise that we'll be okay as long as our beliefs or choices don't clash. Seems reasonable, right? Eliminate discrepancies, eliminate strife?

Adding to this belief is a message often promoted throughout the church, one that can cause significant confusion. Many of our marriages were built on the premise that when the two of us say, "I do," we are to "become one." The words of God on which this view is based have been widely misunderstood and wrongly applied; this has led many people into tremendous frustration and disillusionment. It can put you and your marriage at odds—in a fight—with the truth about life, relationships, and your own humanity.

Intimacy: What It Is, and Isn't

Our ultimate relational goal is birthed in Genesis 2:23–24, where God gives his directives for marriage:

> The man said, "This is now bone of my bones and flesh of my flesh; she shall be called 'woman,' for she was taken out of man." For this reason a man will leave his father and mother and be united to his wife, and they will become one flesh.

Every person was designed for deep, intimate relationship, but people often either have difficulty comprehending or are deeply misled about what this ache in our being is calling for and what true intimacy is. When diagramed, we often find intimacy drawn something like this:

Intimacy?

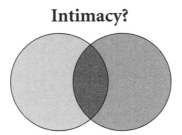

If the two circles signify husband and wife, we are usually taught that intimacy occurs in the overlapping area. One reason this diagram appeals: It illustrates a vital realm of connection and seems to imply a relationship that's growing together. However, this model for "oneness" brings us to an underlying predicament.

If growing together in this way is what we want and what we were made for, then the diagram above does show a relationship making progress. But we're not stretching the model far enough. Consider: If we are attempting to move our marriage from having moments of warm intimacy to the supreme goal of achieving true, constant "oneness," what would that look like?

Oneness?

Perfect intimacy would look like this. Under the common "oneness" model, upon achieving "the goal," we are no longer two—we are now "one." Here again is the big dilemma: We must ask what we have to do to get from intimacy to oneness. In other words, *what do we have to eliminate?*

The Journey?

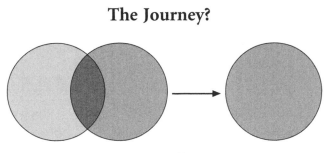

Obstacle = Differences

Under this framework, the obstacle to our intimacy and oneness is individual differences. Therefore, reaching the goal means eliminating the discrepancies so there's no difference between us—the "perfect oneness" that we have understood to mean, essentially, "sameness." The resulting problem is twofold, because (1) differences are intentionally created by God and are a blessing if you know how to use them, and (2) getting rid of them is not possible.

When I take the time to think through this model carefully, it doesn't take long to solve the riddle. Take a minute and imagine what it would be like being married to someone exactly like you. Those who experience ongoing, unresolved dissension may immediately think, *Sounds like the way to go!* In reality, however, unless you have an amazing tolerance for tedium, being married to your clone—even wrapped in the opposite sex—would be horrible. You'd have the exact same thoughts, desires, ideas, feelings ... everything! There'd be nothing to talk about. If that *still* sounds appealing, here's the clincher: If you are both the same, one of you is unnecessary.

In sports, one key to building a great team is finding the ideal combination of distinct gifts and range of strengths brought by the team members. Even though each will also have weaknesses and shortcomings, overall they compensate for one another's limitations. Marriage works on the same principle. I can't tell you the number of couples I meet wherein one spouse is trying to control the other and basically mold or morph the mate into his or her likeness. *The complementary nature of individual character qualities is essential to creating and sustaining interest.*

Music offers another way of looking at the value of differences. Artistic cooperation creates music that's pleasant, textured, and captivating. One person playing a solo instrument can produce pleasing music. A second person playing the same instrument and in unison playing the same notes wouldn't add nearly as much as would a second musician playing a different instrument and different notes in harmony.

Composition and performance that include instrumental variety and rhythmic harmony result in some of the world's most beautiful and appealing music: music that delights us, inspires us, and brings us back to it again and again. The same is possible in marriage; if we're willing to challenge our beliefs about what it means for husband and wife to be one, we can begin to implement a solution that's firmly based in Scripture *and* jibes with our soul.

I love the apostle Paul's brilliant insight about differences:

> The body is a unit, though it is made up of many parts; and though all its parts are many, they form one body. . . . If the foot should say, "Because I am not a hand, I do not belong to the body," it would not for that reason cease to be part of the body. . . . But in fact God has arranged the parts in the body, every one of them, just as he wanted them to be. If they were all one part, where would the body be? . . . The eye cannot say to the hand, "I don't need you!" And the head cannot say to the feet, "I don't need you!" On the contrary, those parts of the body that seem to be weaker are indispensable, and the parts that we think are less honorable we treat with special honor. And the parts that are unpresentable

are treated with special modesty, while our presentable parts need no special treatment. But God has combined the members of the body and has given greater honor to the parts that lacked it, so that there should be no division in the body. (1 Corinthians 12:12, 15, 18–19, 21–25)

Apparently our separate identities were designed to be essential to our overall well-being, not only in our communities but also in our marriages. Diversity is meant to be a blessing to all. The truth is, when individualities themselves appear problematic, there's a real underlying issue: our not knowing how to appreciate and work with them. If we're without a reliable method to make room for and utilize our differences, they will be a complicating nuisance.

To find a fix and discover how to work effectively with differences, we need to first understand and value the beauty of God's individual design. As Paul reminds us, we are created intentionally unique for a reason. Each of us has a boundary that separates us from each other. This boundary establishes our identity as a person; it is *not* to be disregarded or overridden, because we need it for survival, for health, and for wholeness.

Christian belief holds that we will retain our identity for all eternity, that in heaven we will see those whom we have known and loved and they will be recognizable. In contrast, a common belief among many Eastern religions is that our experience of separateness is only an illusion. That we are all part of "universal oneness"—essentially the same—and in the afterlife there will be no separate identity. Accordingly, one of the fundamental paths toward spiritual enlightenment is to *transcend* the illusion and begin experiencing "oneness" here and now. Forgive my vast overgeneralization; my intention here is to point out the contrast. Followers of Jesus believe that our unique identity is *not* an illusion—it exists now and forever.

Our identity is dependent upon having an intact boundary. Ever seen what happens to a single-celled organism when its membrane ruptures? Everything that was contained within the cell diffuses into everything around it. The cell itself ceases to exist.

Keeping the membrane (boundary) intact is an absolute necessity for the cell's life, and there's another critical factor to its staying alive. All living organisms have boundaries that are semi-permeable. In other words, the cell's membrane is solid enough to hold it together, preventing a loss of identity, but it's also designed to allow nutrients in and get waste out. In this way, every living organism has a continual exchange with the environment. Some components are granted access, others must leave or pass through. Still other things (such as, in the body's case, vital organs) are held in place and are meant to stay inside and be protected. This is a consistent and essential blueprint, both physically and relationally, for all living entities.

Whole Person

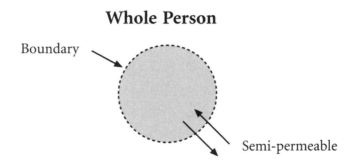

This alternative to the "sameness" definition of intimacy and the "becoming one" precept of closeness upholds and respects the wholeness and uniqueness of each individual. Personal boundaries are to be encouraged and maintained. Each person's invaluable thoughts and feelings are to be protected; this allows him or her to be sufficiently open emotionally, spiritually, mentally and/or physically to invite sharing and connection. This can include getting to know and getting to be known by another.

Deeper forms of relating involve sharing heartfelt thoughts and feelings, which generally means some level of vulnerability. It could be diagrammed like this:

Intimacy

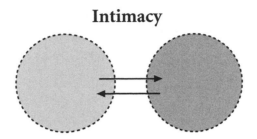

Intimacy, then, is two whole, unique people coming together to share a portion of their innermost self during a trusting exchange. Notice there are no overlapping circles. This does not mean we don't have things in common; it means we remain complete individuals while being intimate, just as God designed us.

The lead character of *Jerry Maguire* is a sports agent who's been successful but has lacked both integrity and a connection to any deeper sense of meaning. After his career collapses, through the journey to rebuild his life, he falls in love with a woman who challenges him to look inside and discover the caring, honorable man he is meant to be. It is Dorothy Boyd's hope that Jerry Maguire will soon discover the true meaning of life, found only in loving and being loved.

Jerry has long had his priorities out of order, and through his relational idiocy he almost loses the very person who motivates him to reclaim his real identity. At the film's climax, when the dramatic tension is at its peak, when it seems the man who hates being alone has inalterably alienated the woman he loves, Jerry sees the light. In a room full of women, he publicly expresses his devotion by saying, "You complete me." All the women melt and swoon.

Not me. I say, "Yuck!"

I understand the sentiment that stirs when Dorothy and her sweet little boy, Ray, prevail in helping Jerry find his heart and the greater sense of being that results from their relationship. I even love that he doesn't want to go through life without her. But the idea that he was incomplete without her is no small slap in the Creator's face. I cannot accept the notion that singles are created to be half-people bumping around without purpose until they find their other puzzle piece.

Jerry is designed to be complete in Christ. Granted, his life is certainly richer and more rewarding with someone to share in his adventure and challenge him to fulfill his potential. However, the notion of one person completing another is among the perilous set-ups that leave couples frustrated and despondent. We humans are not capable of pulling that off. Here's a better expression of relational completeness in a Christ-centered marriage:

Intimate Oneness

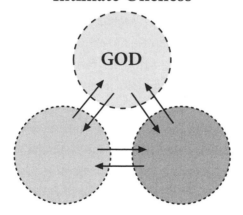

Intimate oneness is radically different from sameness. Oneness occurs when two intimate people also share a common mission, such as being committed to serving God and being conformed to the image of Christ. Like all the body's parts working together toward a common goal—maintaining the body's overall health and well-being—*oneness is about unity of purpose.*

Again the physical body provides a wonderful example. At times a cell or group of cells loses sight of the guiding purpose, which is maintaining the body's overall health, and begins to multiply indiscriminately. These cells can form into tumors and hinder the functioning of vital organs; unaddressed, these mutant cells can take over and destroy the body's life-sustaining systems. This life-threatening condition we call cancer.

To be honest, this concept of oneness, not as sameness but as "unity of purpose," snuck up on me. Before Jenni led me to the Lord, I was fairly independent and headstrong. I had my own ideas and often prided myself on seeing things differently. After coming to Christ, that part of my personality remained.

Jenni is also independent and strong-minded, and she likewise had her own ideas. This led to numerous conflicts of ideas and opinions. Because of how differently we approached life, there were times she would look at how I was attempting to walk out my faith and essentially say, "Bob, if you keep going that way you're not going to get there." I'd look at how she practiced her faith and say the same thing to her. But every so often we'd be wandering along our personal faith-path and bump headlong into each other. This always surprised both of us, and its repeated occurrence caused us to look at each other and say, "I saw where you were going, so how did you get here?"

One day I finally realized that we ended up in the same place because, individually, we each had adopted the same ambition. Each of us had an overarching life goal of becoming increasingly conformed to the image of Christ. Since there is only one image of Christ, as long as we're both heading in that direction we'll ultimately meet along the way. We are "one" in spirit and purpose. In the biblical/physical metaphor, we are both functional parts of the same body, the body of Christ, and we share the ultimate expression of human intimacy and oneness through the committed union of marriage. Thus we are two whole individuals who function as "one flesh." Beautiful, isn't it?

Unity of purpose (biblical oneness) is not trying to become one by getting rid of differences but learning how to value and utilize those differences for the "team's" overall well-being, assisting each other in moving together toward the desired destination. Intimate oneness in a Christ-centered marriage includes two people who choose to open themselves to each other and share themselves and their lives (the inward and outward journeys), while each nurtures an intimate relationship with God, doing the same thing with him.

One of a couple's biggest challenges: Seeing the differences between them as the problem to be solved tends to make the marriage feel crowded, as if there isn't really enough room for both to be the fullest expression of who they were created to be. The marriage is significantly blessed when both are committed to making sure that each is encouraged and able to *aspire*. That's a relationship with plenty of breathing room.

I don't want Jenni to feel stifled or limited in any way as a person. This is not to suggest that the goal is taking license to do anything we want without commitment to the team. The fact that being on the same team means being all we're meant to be individually is *also* for the good of the team. A mutually satisfying marriage feels roomy enough for two. If you construct it to feel crowded, someone will begin to feel suffocated, restricted, and increasingly gasping for fresh air.

Marriage: Three Essential, Vital, Simultaneous Journeys

When our eldest son, Chris, decided to get married, he and our future daughter-in-law, Amara, asked if I'd be willing to perform the ceremony. I agreed, and we began to discuss what they had in mind and what special details they'd include. Both mentioned wanting to use the lighting of a unity candle as a symbol of their transition from being separate individuals to becoming a joined couple.

This ceremony typically involves two candles representing two people and a larger third (unity) candle in the middle, representing their marriage. The mothers of the bride and groom would come onto the platform and light the candle of their child, symbolizing and honoring the mother's role in bringing the new life into being. I was then to take the two candles and use them, simultaneously, to light the center candle, representing the marriage as a new life.

Commonly, the pastor then blows out the two individual candles, the still-lit unity candle symbolizing that the bride and groom, no longer separate, are now "one." When I see this, my hair stands on end, and I'm tempted to jump up and yell, "No, don't do that to those poor unsuspecting people!" I told Chris and his beautiful fiancée I would only participate in this ceremony if after lighting the unity candle I did not blow out the two individual candles. Why? On the day we become married we do not stop being distinct entities. *We do not* subtract *individual identities; we* add *a new living entity.*

A healthy, vibrant marriage consists of three fully lit candles— concurrent journeys that all must be attended to and nurtured.

The first candle represents your journey in being the fullest expression of who you were created to be; your health and well-being are incredibly important to God, and so should they be to you.

Second, your spouse's candle must burn brightly while becoming the fullest expression of his or her true self. To have a successful, satisfying, and meaningful shared life, both people must be cared for and nurtured throughout their lives.

Once two journeys join together in marriage, a new flame sparks to life. No longer are there just the separate Bob and Jenni journeys. We have a third, together. Simply caring for the two individuals does not assure that the marriage will be healthy and alive, just as caring for the marriage will not assure that the individuals will feel healthy and alive. I can grow and develop as a person, and so can Jenni, but our relationship will only grow and develop to the degree we invest in it also. In order for all three journeys to thrive, they all need and deserve constant care and attention.

All for One: Becoming Teammates

No one can defeat us unless we first defeat ourselves.
—Dwight D. Eisenhower

If these goals—becoming one in spirit and purpose and having a marriage with plenty of room for both people—sound at all appealing, then becoming full partners and teammates will be a breath of fresh air! When I married Jenni I mistakenly thought I was marrying my fantasy happily-ever-after partner; I eventually came to recognize that I'd actually chosen my real-life "journeying" partner. Our shared adventure is amazing, full of exhilaration and unexpected challenges. Our shared romance is engaging, fascinating, and highly satisfying, even with all we still don't know and understand. One thing I know for sure: We are partners on this sojourn, committed to being true to ourselves, to God, to each other, and to our marriage. We are teammates and allies, "all for one and one for all."

In *The DNA of Relationships*[1] and *The DNA of Relationships for Couples*,[2] we wrote about the importance of recognizing that marriage is like a team sport. You either win as a team or lose as a team; when you're on the same team, there are only two possible outcomes: *You both win, or you both lose.* Period. Unfortunately, for many years I never applied this simple principle to my marriage and thus was continually frustrated and disappointed. I had succumbed to the illusion that there could be one winner and one loser.

In our early years, when Jenni and I entered a conflict or power struggle, we'd allow ourselves to become postured as opponents and even enemies. We didn't yet know how to apply the wisdom of Luke 11:17, where Jesus says, "A house divided against itself will fall." Since then we've learned firsthand that a team with ego-driven infighting and poor cooperation is not likely to come away with a championship.

I like to play hard and triumph, and I especially like to play on winning teams. More important, I want my marriage to be a winning team. Therefore, no matter how upset I become over an issue, or how wronged I might feel before we reach resolve, I can't ever allow myself to see Jenni as the enemy; she is always my teammate and partner. No matter how much I disagree at the moment, I can never promote fighting, with or without rules. For either of us to win—and, thus, for our team to win—both of us must feel great about where we end up. (Note for those in abusive relationships: Before teamwork can work for you, some key elements from chapter 6, "Protect—Your Place of Refuge," must first be in place.)

Once I had my eyes opened to this truth I began to discover a simple key to victory. I wanted our marriage to be great for both of us, and the only way for us to have a win all the way around was by embracing an entirely new paradigm for resolving disagreements. In our home, for everything from basic decisions to passionate differences in perspective (which can easily escalate into full-blown war zones), we adopted a "no-losers policy." In other words, we agreed that it was unacceptable for either of us to walk away from any situation with one or both of us feeling defeated. There are few relational principles with more power to change forever the course of a marriage than this one.

This is not to say that defeat isn't possible for our team. Either of us can torpedo the team at any time and cause a loss. It's taken time for me to realize that when I felt I was winning and Jenni was losing, we *both* took a hit and lost. Other times I wouldn't be trying to win as much as trying not to lose; nevertheless, I still treated Jenni as my opponent. Even though these didn't *feel* like team losses, once I realized what was happening, none of it was okay with me anymore. If the team suffered a loss, I was determined to find ways to keep it from happening again. Losses became unacceptable, and I sought to do everything *within my power* to set us up for victory.

Over time this change in attitude alone began to make a difference in our marriage. I now understand what changed so dramatically with Jenni and me. In the past, when we'd get snagged over a disagreement, we'd both adopt a posture or stance of battle-readiness, or at least defensiveness. We were bracing for a fight, preparing to pounce or feel trounced again. Now when we bump into a possible conflict that needs attention, the first thing I say to Jenni is something like this:

> Before we talk about the issue I want you to know that I won't accept any solution unless you like it. I won't try to talk you into anything or sell you on it. Either it works for you or it doesn't work for me.

I've realized that if my wife isn't good with the decision, she will feel like she's taken a loss. At first, I had to really stay on my game so she could begin to trust that I wouldn't work a quick maneuver. With time, Jenni has experienced my living up to these words enough to know I mean it. As a result, she doesn't feel she has to watch her back with me anymore. She no longer worries about my trying to steamroll or wear her down in an attempt to get my way. As the concern about losing has left our relationship, she and I have felt safe enough to allow our hearts and spirits to remain open and available; that's the state we need to occupy in order to receive a creative and inspired alternative.

Jenni and I are just as individual as ever, but we can now work through stuff so fast it's often as if the conflict weren't even there.

This is important to note, because the most common concern I hear is that while adopting a no-losers policy sounds great in theory, couples fear it will take too much time before it works. I have found exactly the opposite to be true. We have saved literally months of frustration, yelling, silence, distance, and perpetually feeling like losers. Even if learning and applying your own no-losers policy does take extra time and effort in the beginning, possible success is better than certain failure, and in the end, regardless, it takes much less time. I'll walk you through "Seven Steps to a Win/Win Solution" in chapter 10.

In order to adopt this policy in your relationship you must be willing and prepared to walk into the face of uncertainty. Over the years, *hundreds* of times I've encountered issues in my marriage that on the front side looked impossible. Everything in me wanted to take control and try to create a solution on my own. Adopting a no-losers policy requires a willingness to find enough faith to walk into the adventure of an uncertain outcome and trust that God will see you through successfully.

Can you believe that God is a God of unity, and that he is committed and available to help you get there? If you'll let him be your guide, you can find the courage to take the walk. Regarding the countless apparently insurmountable differences Jenni and I (as well as each of our children) have faced, I'm thankful to be able to report that with God's help, a desire to win, and a commitment to the team, we've been able to find our way through every one. I consider this a testimony to God's faithfulness and perfect love.

Conclusion

Before setting about outlining and scripting an adventurous plot, a novelist often looks for characters that are seemingly worlds apart. The son of the mob don falls in love with the daughter of an FBI agent. The prince is enamored with a slave girl. An ex-con marries a preacher's daughter. Differences bring about the spark of captivating interest. Rather than trying to rid ourselves of differences in the search for unity, we can find that our comfortable yoke is to be worn instead with common purpose—our eyes and our lives set on our Savior and Redeemer (see Matthew 11:29). When we commit to winning together, at last we can know true victory.

———————— *to* **Ponder** *and* **Discuss** ————————

1. What do you see as differences between you and your spouse? What do you see as similarities?

2. How have your differences made your relationship more difficult or enhanced your relationship?

3. Before reading this chapter, what did you think it meant to become "one" in marriage?

4. If you were to define oneness as "unity of purpose," would anything change in how your marriage functions?

5. When you have conflict with your spouse, do you typically feel like an adversary or a teammate? Describe the last time you felt like a team.

6. Is your team a winning team or a losing team? How does your spouse assess it?

7. What would change about how you participate in your relationship if a no-losers policy was the norm for you and your spouse?

CHAPTER 6

— PROTECT —
Your Place of Refuge

*Oh, the comfort, the inexpressible comfort of feeling safe
with a person, having neither to weigh thoughts nor
measure words, but pouring them all out, just as they are,
chaff and grain together, certain that a faithful hand will
take and sift them, keep what is worth keeping, and with a
breath of kindness blow the rest away.*
—George Eliot

Once a couple makes the move to being allies, the scene is set to create their own relational sanctuary, a place of intimate refuge and protection. The presence of your spouse should feel like the safest place in the world. When we hear the word *safety*, we probably first think of being physically sheltered, but I'd like to expand this to include relational safety.

Allow your mind to wander back to a time when you felt warm, treasured, protected, or secure. How old were you? What was the circumstance, and who was with you? Now compare that sensation to how you feel when you're with your spouse. Do you feel relaxed and open? On the flip side, have you ever felt remorse after lashing out, being insensitive, or somehow compromising your spouse's trust? I have, and I don't want it to happen again.

One of the many times I tore a hole in the sanctuary of my marriage occurred on Christmas Eve several years ago. Jenni and I had planned some last-minute shopping in a neighboring town about forty-five miles away. That morning when I checked the weather report I was surprised to hear a snowstorm was on its way and would arrive around 5:00 P.M. When I told Jenni, she became a little hesitant about going. I, on the other hand, wasn't at all concerned because I was sure we could make it back with plenty of time before the snow started. "Let's see," I said with marked confidence. "It's nine now, and we can get out of the house by ten. We'll be there and back by noon—one at the latest. No sweat. We'll beat the storm by a good four or five hours."

Jenni reluctantly agreed, and once we were in motion we looked like contestants on *The Amazing Race.* We had our shopping done and were en route back home as planned. I was busy patting us both on the back when I turned on the radio. The announcer's voice cut to a special weather brief. I paused and gave a quick glance in Jen's direction. The weather guy was putting out a storm warning due to blizzard-like conditions in Branson, our hometown. I craned my neck toward the dashboard and studied the sky in disbelief. It was still mostly clear. And it was only noon. There had to be a mistake. But five miles later we were into a storm so intense it was nearly a whiteout.

Not only had I talked my wife into this trip against her better judgment, but she and I have very different ideas about the proper way to drive in snow. Ever have a difference with your spouse about driving? Jenni believes (1) you can never be too safe, (2) you can never drive too slowly, and (3) you can never be too far back from the car in front of you. Like many guys, I want to feel the vehicle's back end fishtail just a little so I can get a good feel for the road and assess how bad the conditions really are. Jenni immediately let me know she had a difference of perspective. Of course, my sensitive response was, "Ah, honey, I've got things totally under control; just relax and we'll be fine."

By this time whiteness pummeled down in blinding sheets. Even I was becoming a bit concerned. With more vigor Jenni made her opinion known. "Bob, slow down!"

I slowed down. Then she said it again, so I slowed down even more. After her third outburst, I retorted with something about being able to walk home faster than we were driving. With a steel grip on her door handle, her eyes stayed glued to the windshield.

"Bob you're too close to that car."

I backed off, but she still wasn't happy. Her agitation growing, she continued "helping me" drive until I finally growled through clenched teeth, "Jenni, I am at least thirty car lengths behind that truck."

The tension continued to build, and I was reminded to keep both hands on the wheel. We were now in the middle of a swirling, frozen tundra, surrounded by nothing but trees and wilderness. At the rate we were going, I figured we wouldn't be home before the spring thaw. I was creeping along, dozens of car lengths behind the closest vehicle with my hands locked in the ten-and-two.

It still was not good enough for Jen. All of a sudden she exploded. Slapping her knees, she started screaming at the top of her lungs, "I FEEL LIKE I'M GOING TO DIE! PULL THIS CAR OVER RIGHT NOW AND LET ME OUT. I'M WALKING HOME!"

Do you think it makes me a bad person if for a split second I actually considered it? But I couldn't figure out how I'd explain to the kids why Mommy wasn't home on Christmas Eve. And then a vision of the newspaper byline flashed in my mind: "Local marriage expert abandons wife on roadside during the worst recorded blizzard in history."

All humor aside, Jenni finally had my full attention. Neurotic? Yes. Unreasonable? Most likely. But in that moment I realized that my wife was terrified . . . and felt totally unsafe with me. She had completely closed down, and as a result there was no intimacy between us. Nor for that matter was there likely to be any later that night.

Obviously we can't control all the many variables that can threaten our security (such as the heavens opening up and dumping out rain or snow). And we can't force other people to act according to our desires. However, we can, as a couple, determine what being in relationship with each other will be like. We prefer to feel safe and secure. Our hearts have a natural default setting to be open to each other—we just want to know we won't regret it later.

If you want a trusting, intimate relationship and all its accompanying benefits, you must make safety a central focus of your home. Together, you can commit to creating a hedge of protection around your marriage so that regardless of what happens in this crazy, mixed-up world you'll rest assured that your marriage is a safe haven, your place of refuge. The first step in making this a reality is noticing the degree to which it may be missing in your marriage and recognizing its importance.

Few couples, even those with good marriages, report feeling completely secure (emotionally, spiritually, mentally, and physically) with their spouse. Very few experience the presence of their spouse as a place without fear of judgment, criticism, rejection, withdrawal, indifference, and so on. One reason for this: Husbands and wives rarely if ever discuss their individual need for safety within the relationship, let alone feel empowered in making relational safety a defining characteristic of their home.

Typically, when looking for ways to overcome obstacles to having the marriage of our dreams, we take on one of the two areas most likely to need improvement: *creating intimacy* or *creating openness.*

We know we want more passion and a deeper connection, so we try to figure out how to get them. Maybe we haven't been spending enough time together, so we schedule a date night. We might recognize the need for better communication, so we go to the bookstore and thumb through the wall of books on active listening. In doing so, you'll learn that *the attempt to create intimacy guarantees tons of work and is much harder than necessary.*

Or, we see that barriers erected in the relationship are closing us off from our loved one. At some level we know that real intimacy and connection require the relationship to be open, and more openness leads to more intimacy, right? We reason that we need to obliterate any bars or barricades around our hearts so that nothing's guarded or buffered. You will soon find, though, that inevitable inner turmoil ensues and that *trying to pry open yourself or your spouse generally feels uncaring, uncomfortable, or just plain dangerous.*

Self-Protection

There's a better and less onerous way to the marriage of your dreams, one that merely involves grasping a basic tenet of human nature.

God created us with a profound survival instinct—we are naturally inclined toward self-protection. We prefer to avoid danger and pain, both physically and emotionally, and fear alerts us to the possibility of their presence. When we feel in any way at risk or threatened we feel some form of fear; our body responds according to the strength of the emotion. We know the natural reaction to fear is either to fight or to flee. Both are part of our divinely endowed self-protection system and are integral to our ultimate survival.

A fear response may involve a small degree of concern, leading one to being more alert and vigilant. Or, it could convey a full-on state of emergency in which one must ready for battle by hunkering down, closing up, and preparing to fight or take flight. In either case the fear itself is not wrong or bad; it's only an emotion triggered to ensure survival. *Nevertheless, fear is fundamentally anti-relational.*

Remember, intimacy occurs while hearts are open and shared. The state of openness brings an intrinsic degree of vulnerability and, therefore, involves a measure of danger and risk. Caring about and opening your heart to a person exposes you to the possibility of being hurt or rejected.

As such, it's normal to be reluctant about entering headlong into an intimate relationship. Some choose to avoid risk altogether. Those of us who want to experience the joys of intimacy find ourselves seeking to balance handling the internal conflict while at the same time trying to play it safe. The result: We don't know if we're advancing or retreating.

Honoring Walls

Most people I know view emotional walls, like silence, as unfortunate obstacles that keep them from experiencing the levels of intimacy they desire. Thus, wanting to get rid of the protective obstructions, they set about building a strategy to tear them down. But the walls, rather than disappearing, get higher and thicker; the suddenly vulnerable heart, feeling frighteningly exposed and unjustifiably at risk, wants to pull away. Think for a moment about why these walls are erected. Always installed by one who doesn't feel safe and secure, dividers are put in place to shelter the heart that feels vulnerable to hurt.

When Jenni would build a wall between us, I hated it. I couldn't understand her motive. Sometimes she'd become cold and distant while hiding behind the barrier. Other times, feeling more directly threatened, she'd become irritable and angry while shooting arrows at the intruder. Sadly, I thought she was just being difficult and unreasonable. I knew I wasn't going to hurt her, and I was confident we'd be able to enjoy connecting if she'd only give me a chance.

Armed with high-road self-righteousness and the firm belief that I was doing what was ultimately best for both of us, I did everything I knew to remove the walls of defense around her heart. No strategy went untried. I attempted to blast them down. I tried dismantling them stone by stone. I tunneled under. I scaled over. I tried sweetly persuading her to open the doors. As a last exasperated effort, I'd get angry and shame her for not cooperating. (No wonder she didn't trust me!)

At some point I had a powerful revelation about walls and safety. I came to see that she had her defenses up with me because she didn't trust me. She was afraid if she let me in, I could and would hurt her. I realized that when I went after her walls I only confirmed everything she feared. I was doing a bang-up job of proving to her that I was unsafe. In that life-changing epiphany, I knew I hadn't really cared about how she felt.

As you know, early in our marriage we had lots of battles. Whenever I'd get upset, I'd have one standout issue I'd want to address more than any other—typically it had to do with something *she* did, and what I wanted *her* to change. For some strange reason Jenni never enjoyed those conversations! After several rounds of my heavy-handed attempts to help her identify and solve her problem, she'd be so beaten down that all she wanted was to get away. When she left whatever room we'd been in, what do you think I'd do? Yep. I'd follow her. She'd go from room to room, trying to escape me, until finally one day she went into the bathroom and locked the door.

This looked like a great opportunity—I now had a captive audience. I figured I'd be there awhile, so I leaned against the molding and slid down to the floor, thinking I might as well be comfortable. I kept up the barrage, talking right through the door. Though Jenni wasn't responding, I knew she could hear me, so I continued until I heard the car start outside in the driveway. My captive audience had literally climbed through the window to escape me.

———

In hindsight, long after the rush of anger and humiliation, I think what my wife did was awesome. In no way was I safe for her at that moment, and she took great care of herself. I've come to realize that her emotional and physical well-being must not be compromised. She is capable of being hurt, and I am capable of hurting her.

Finally I made a choice to care more about the person behind the wall than I did about getting what I wanted. I would honor not only her but the walls too. I let Jenni know that her not trusting me was important and that it saddened me. I didn't want anything or anyone to hurt her, especially me.

I told her I wouldn't try to get her to take the walls down, and that I'd be thankful she was safe. Though I was disappointed we weren't able to connect the way I wanted to, her well-being was more important. I wanted to be her protector, not a threat.

———

This change in attitude made a marked impact on Jenni. Because people don't like living in isolation, and because most want to have a vibrant marriage, we will usually begin to lower the walls once we know we won't regret it—once we experience marriage as a sanctuary.

Openness requires much less energy than trying to protect one-self, so openness leaves more energy for living, loving, and learning. We all prefer to be open and relaxed as long as we're confident we won't get hurt. When two people feel genuinely safe and secure together, they'll naturally begin to open up because it's easier—we're designed to do so. *Since intimacy is nothing more than two people with open hearts sharing something of each other with each other, openness together creates an intimate connection.*

If a marital sanctuary sounds appealing to you, it's critical you understand that the feeling of safety in marriage is extremely fragile; it's easy to damage and difficult to restore. Sadly, many people don't recognize this and as a result are lazy or careless. When they're thoughtless or insensitive, they act as if everything will be (and should be) restored if they only apologize. Nothing could be further from the truth.

An apology, even coupled with sincere repentance, can lead to genuine forgiveness from and healing in your spouse; *still,* the safety of the environment has been compromised. Openness and intimacy remain available, just more difficult. Even occasional insensitivity causes us to be cautious and wary. Each time safety is compromised we'll be less confident about the future. In order for us to be able to relax without being continually on guard, we need to be assured that we're valued and will continue to be safe.

Remember how we used to wander freely through airports and have family and friends accompany us to the gate to say good-bye? Tragic events in our nation's recent past have caused us to be in a continual state of collective alert. Security has tightened; we must anticipate what might happen next. I've become accustomed to the routine and all the extra inconveniences now apparently necessary to assure our safety. But I'm also very aware that because of past breaches, we may never again enjoy feeling relaxed in an airport without extreme protective measures in place.

This same ambience can become the norm in a marriage as well. The repetition of small insensitivities and carelessness causes bruises and wounds. Over time, this results in an adjustment that means we no longer feel relaxed in our marriage environment without extreme protective measures in place. The good news is, in contrast to air travel, which can involve countless possible threats, your marriage only has two variables: you and your spouse. If the two of you commit to (1) recognizing the importance of carefully protecting your marital environment and (2) working to restore a safe haven anytime it's been compromised, your marriage can begin to feel secure.

Life's Greatest Treasure

Before we discuss safety in the context of marriage, let's be clear what it is we want to be safe. What is it I'm trying to protect? I've come to understand that safety has everything to do with my heart—that part of me where the *life-treasure* from God resides. I probably best comprehend this part of who I am when I think of a newborn infant.

I have four children and was fortunate to be present at each of their births. On each occasion I was overwhelmed at the miracle of life. When holding that squirming, wrinkled-up little person, I am struck with the inadequacy of language to describe the worth of human life. Not just in general, but of this particular child. With my own children I cannot possibly put into words how valuable that essence of life is to me.

This preciousness is even more remarkable in light of how a baby's desirability is not consistent with most of our conventions about what makes a person valuable. A newborn hasn't yet exhibited any special talents or accomplished any heroic feats. Even though there might be cheers going up for that first poopy, it hardly ranks as a value-enhancing performance. Neither are infants especially known for their physical beauty. But the parents revere and cherish no one on the face of the earth so much as that tiny baby.

The Bible informs us that God formed Adam and Eve from the dust of the ground. It has been said that the cost of the water and minerals that make up the material of the human body probably wouldn't amount to more than $40. So where does this worth originate? What is the source of such wonder and awe? *It is the breath of God himself.* It is the Creator's breath within us and the value he has imparted to us.

In addition to what preciousness we ascribe to the human heart in considering the indescribable, eternal value of a newborn babe, we gain insight into our innate worth through our knowledge of how immensely vulnerable an infant is. Many parents can attest to the overwhelming sense of responsibility they felt when holding their child for the first time. This brand-new little person is dependent upon parents for its very survival, so fragile that he or she requires constant care and monitoring. The delicate breath of life in those first weeks relies fully upon provision, nurture, and attention.

In recent years I've had a vivid awareness that I came into the world in just the same way as my children; my parents held me with that same mix of emotions. Furthermore, my children are no less valuable to me today than the day they were born, and I understand that even though they're learning and growing in their capacity to fend for themselves, they will always have a heart that can be injured if I'm not careful and sensitive.

This is what we're talking about when we speak of safety in relationships (generally) and in marriage (specifically): the heart, the life-treasure resident within us, representing both our eternal value and our immediate vulnerability. When we're born, caring for this treasure is a responsibility given to our parents. Some are blessed with parents who understand our value and vulnerability; others had parents who didn't always or often treat us accordingly. Neither alters our value or vulnerability, even though the latter may have left us confused as to our worth. In either case, heart care is no longer our parents' job. At some point, responsibility to be the steward of my heart is mine to accept and embrace.

What does stewardship of the heart mean? The authors of *Behind the Bottom Line,*[1] a book outlining Christian business principles, define a steward as "someone who protects and adds value to assets that are not their own." The life-treasure within me is not of my own making. It was placed there by none other than God Almighty. God himself is asking me to be the steward of that treasure, to be caretaker of my own heart. The value of who I am and the vulnerability I live with every day are my responsibility.

Safety for Two Can Start With One

If I ask, "Do you feel safe in your marriage?" what's the first thing that comes to mind? Most of us, if we're honest, admit we translate this as "Does my spouse make me feel secure?" We're inclined to think of safety as comfort provided by our spouse. I suggest to you that there are at least two ways I can go about establishing and maintaining protection in my marriage entirely on my own, without any input from my spouse.

Here is where I first impact the safety of my marriage. In this relationship, what kind of job am I doing at being a steward of my own heart? How do I attend and care for this priceless treasure God has placed within me? My initial responsibility in establishing and maintaining safety in my marriage is with my own heart. If that sounds self-centered, consider: How can we love another if we've not first loved ourselves?

As I watch my adult children making their way in the world and engaging in intimate relationships, I pray that they will continually recognize how valuable they are and treat themselves accordingly. When they don't treat themselves well—emotionally, physically, mentally, or spiritually—my heart breaks. I often feel helpless because they're now adults, responsible for themselves, but as a loving father I want my precious ones provided for.

I could easily say to them, "Please treat yourself better than that. You deserve more. Don't you know how valuable you are?" I pray they will expect to be treated by others in a way that reflects the concern and protection that they deserve: in fact, the kind of thoughtfulness they give themselves. Jesus said the second part of the greatest commandment is to love others in a way that resembles how you care for yourself (Luke 10:27).

Much of marriage's pain and heartache is a consequence of poor stewardship over one's own heart. Some throw their heart at their spouse, demanding that he or she take the responsibility. Others, after being hurt, hide their heart and then wonder why they don't feel close to their mate. Still others lose contact with their heart altogether without realizing that they're neglected and exposed, perhaps even being perplexed at the constant ache they feel or the restlessness they can't seem to calm. These are just a few of the ways we can fail to protect the life-treasure held in our hearts. I can tell you this: When husbands and wives accept and embrace the wondrous treasure God has placed within them, their lives change.

Just as important as managing my own heart is the posture I take toward Jenni's. She too is priceless and vulnerable—worthy of all the respect and sensitivity I can deliver. I essentially seek to stand in a position of trustworthiness with her, not because I'm responsible for her but because I know her value. Understanding how delicate and beautiful the heart is means I recognize the treasure entrusted to me.

Imagine a friend letting you hold a family heirloom, an irreplaceable, priceless antique. What kind of care would you take as you held it in your hands? What would be the impact on the safety of your marriage if you took that same attitude toward and care with your spouse's desires and concerns?

So we have two reliable ways of establishing safety in marriage, and neither requires action from our spouse. First we ask, "What kind of care am I giving my own heart?" Second, "What posture do I take toward my partner's heart?" *When two hearts are being valued and attended to, the relationship will soon become a sanctuary of warmth and comfort.*

Caring Is the Key

Have a heart that never hardens, a temper that never tires, and a touch that never hurts.
—Charles Dickens

Have you ever wondered if "being in love for a lifetime" is a recent American ideal or, at best, another fantasy? I have. When we examine matrimony around the world we don't hear as much about "in love-ness." It's the practical, utilitarian purpose of marriage that seems to have taken precedence throughout human history. In spite of all the cultural traditions centered on arranged marriages and functional need, however, I find a marriage based on love to have strong biblical merit. Of course there is the perfect love story in Eden, but what about after the fall? Look closely at the whole of Scripture and see that everything in existence exists because of God's love. God *himself* is love (1 John 4:8).

If love is at the center of marriage, we can reason that God is there at the center too. But it gets better. If love is at the center of marriage, marriage is then a matter of the heart. Over 950 Bible verses refer to the heart, which we noted in chapter 1 is "the well-spring of life" (Proverbs 4:23). We open our heart to let God reside there, and then we allow his love to flow in and through us, extending outward to a world desperately in need of it.

If I want my marriage to be more than a short-lived period of "in love-ness"—if I want it to reflect the Creator—then I must see

Jenni as God sees her. I want to feel about her as he does. I want to care about her and be as committed to her and her well-being as he is. I have a tall order to fill; he promises he will never leave or forsake her (Joshua 1:5; Hebrews 13:5). Everything he does is good for her. He *died* for her. I'm convinced that caring is at the heart of Christ; it *is* the heart of Christ. I want everything I am and all that I do to be directed and controlled by love rather than its opposite, which is fear (1 John 4:18).

For a marriage to thrive, two hearts must be skillfully cared for. One of the primary ways I'm able to show and express my care for my wife is in responding to and handling her feelings. I've had clients say something like this: "I know my husband cares about me, but without being aware of it he often uses a patronizing tone and expression that, if the words were taken out, would sound like 'Why do you have to be so stupid?'" The fact is, if I in any way communicate that I think someone's thoughts or feelings are wrong or stupid, he or she will feel uncared for.

Feeling loved involves more than simply knowing one's well-being is covered; one must know and hear that you care about his or her feelings. What you do and say carries heavy and lasting impact. Sometimes people don't realize they're using a patronizing tone, even to themselves. Many have grown up talking so disrespectfully to themselves that they don't even hear their scathing tone. We must continually invest in becoming more skilled at caring for feelings—ours *and* others'.

You can care about how someone feels even if you don't understand why he or she feels that way. You can care about how another feels even if you respond differently. In fact, you can care even if those feelings come from false or irrational beliefs. I was convinced that during that snowstorm Jenni was safe while driving with me and that she was overreacting, but so what? She was genuinely frightened. It was real fear, and that matters to me.

Caring does not require an understanding of why, nor does it require agreement. It doesn't even suggest that you believe the feelings reflect a true or rational perspective. When someone begins to experience that you are genuinely interested in how he or she feels, aside from any other logical reason, he or she often stops being concerned about being right and frequently becomes interested in how you feel.

Most people prefer to care about others; they struggle when they feel they have to watch out for themselves because no one else will. When working with couples at an impasse on a particular topic, we have been repeatedly amazed at how often they find satisfying resolution by having their feelings validated and tended to gently, *even without coming to an agreement.* Over and over we witness astounding breakthroughs in previously icy and distant marriages. When individuals know their feelings will be respected, they feel safe to open up and stay open, which then allows them to reach out and connect intimately.

I hope you will make creating a safe haven your foundational commitment, "the rule of your day." You and your spouse deserve the same level of care and recognition of the God-given value you received when you were newly born. If you didn't receive this care when you were little, it's important you know that you deserved it then and you deserve it today!

A Sacred Privilege

Once you fully appreciate the individual value of your spouse and the foundation of safety is established, you have taken great strides toward creating an environment that can foster a move into enjoying deeper levels of intimacy and connection. At this point you are no longer walled out of your spouse's heart, but you've not yet gained entrance to his or her inner sanctum—the private realm of dreams, passions, and beliefs. Most of us have endured the devastating, humiliating experience of having something deeply personal about us inappropriately shared by someone else. From what we've discussed, you can envision how damaging this could be to the safety of any relationship.

Beyond just encouraging you to be careful with your spouse's personal information, I want to challenge you to think about it differently. My good friend Gary Smalley used to do a presentation on the topic of honor wherein he passed around an old, beat-up violin with its bridge broken and strings hanging off. The audience was told to look at it as it passed. He would ask the group what they thought of the instrument, and then he'd ask if their feelings would change if they were to discover it was a Stradivarius (it was) valued at over $100,000. People would gasp and instantly express different feelings about the old violin. They'd also handle it with much more care.

All of us are like that violin; we all have aspects of infinite worth that should not be handled without the handler's recognition of the value and pledge of utmost care. The private sanctum of our beings deserves and needs utmost respect and care. Our most intimate thoughts must be regarded as the sacred privilege, never the right, of another.

I enter into Jenni's private inner world by invitation only. Being her husband does not give me the right to plow in at my discretion. When I'm in her "holy of holies," I must remember it's an honor that can be revoked at any time, at her volition. Any information I acquire while in that place needs to be handled tenderly and with absolute confidence. If I fail to comply, she has every right and responsibility to restrict my access until I prove to her my trustworthiness with that privilege. When I take this attitude and approach toward my wife, she feels significantly safer and thus more willing to open up and share with me. That has a great payoff for me too because I want to be intimate with her.

This is a challenge for all of us, but you can imagine how being a public figure whose job spins on the axis of writing and talking about marriage can have the potential of making things a little dicey at home. Every day I share details about myself, my marriage, and my wife. Yet I assure you that I take very seriously this responsibility of storytelling while protecting my wife's privacy. Jenni and I have had many a dialogue about which stories she is comfortable with me sharing. Since I have the microphone, I try to keep the illustrations more about my own shortcomings (always plenty to choose from!) while always considering Jenni's part in the story.

A couple of years ago we were lying in bed talking before falling asleep, and this issue once again weighed heavy on my heart. I asked Jenni for the umpteenth time how she was feeling about what I was sharing publicly. My wife, a remarkable woman, fully devoted to our ministry, paused for a moment and said, "Bob, there must have been a reason we went through all that 'yuck' we endured, and if sharing it can help anybody heal from their own pain or avoid it altogether, then you can share whatever you want." I was again impressed with her desire to participate in healing marriages, but I assure you that if ever she changes her mind, I'll honor it, and if she ever doesn't want me to share a particular story or detail, I won't. I'll never forget the sacred privilege I have of knowing her— one that, earlier in our marriage, I almost lost.

Conclusion

The benefits of sanctuary to the soul are essential for both husband and wife to enter into adventure and to enjoy romance. The presence of one's spouse should feel like the safest place in the world. Marriage is ultimately a matter of the heart, and for intimacy to thrive, two hearts must be skillfully protected. Caring is the underlying key to maintaining this safe place; as you both learn to hold gently your sacred privilege, your marriage will become a treasured heirloom to pass on for your children and your children's children.

——————— *to* **Ponder** *and* **Discuss** ———————

1. Discuss the definition of *safe* as described in this chapter.

2. What do you see as the difference between physical, emotional, spiritual, and intellectual safety?

3. Describe a time in your life when you felt memorably safe with someone (parent, grandparent, friend, etc.).

4. Overall, on a scale of 1–10, how safe a person do you think you are for your spouse (1 being unsafe, 10 being totally safe)? On the same 1–10 scale, ask how safe your spouse feels with you emotionally, physically, spiritually, and intellectually.

5. Have you attempted to bring emotional safety to your relationship? If this topic seems new to you, how might you begin to be a safe or safer person for your spouse?

6. When you feel threatened or uneasy in a conflict, are you more prone toward fight or flight (e.g., arguing or withdrawing)? Explain.

7. How do you handle your own heart—the life-treasure God has placed in you—within your marriage? Is your heart accessible; is it hidden; is it thrown at your spouse for him/her to take care of? How well do you care for your heart?

CHAPTER 7

—INTRIGUE—
The Quest for Knowledge

For my part I know nothing with certainty,
but the sight of the stars makes me dream.
—Vincent Van Gogh

Gift giving and receiving is a skill at which I really stink. By Gary Chapman's measure of the love languages, gifts are at the bottom of my list.[1] I've been so bad at receiving presents that Jenni has had to coach me over the years; I frequently hurt the kids' feelings at Christmas. Over time I've learned how to show excitement and exclaim, "Wow, this is great! Boy, could I use this. . . ." Still, my response tends to feel more playacted than sincere. When I want something I go out and get it; the thought never crosses my mind to put it on a wish list as an idea for my family.

I'm not much better at giving material expressions of my

affection. I get anxious when trying to come up with an item for someone I love—especially Jenni. I love her so much, and I want her to be excited about my gifts. Unfortunately, my mind just doesn't think that way, and my amorous gestures commonly land with a thud. One year for Mother's Day, as I was wandering through the store, a shiny item caught my eye and reminded me of a pleasant childhood memory Jenni had once shared. It involved fond moments when she and her family would make big breakfasts together, with a special toaster. . . . What luck! I was looking right at an unusually attractive four-slice model.

When Sunday arrived, the kids were all wound up and couldn't wait to honor Mommy with their tokens of love. Jenni opened all the kids' packages and, as always, loved everything they gave her. I was apprehensive yet hopeful that mine might spark a warm memory *and* produce some delicious toast.

Last to open was the carefully wrapped box I'd set before her. When the beautiful Sunbeam came free of its wrapping, I could see she was struggling with how to respond. She glanced at the floor for an instant, gathering her thoughts. Her somewhat forced smile and gracious "thank you" let me know instantly that once again I'd somehow missed the mark. Even my attempt to remind her of her childhood didn't get me there. I've since come to learn that appliances rarely make romantic gifts and perhaps might even send the unfortunate message of wanting to equip the "little woman" for her job at home. (Not at all my intent.)

I was about to learn a valuable lesson. That same day a good friend of ours called to give Jenni some good news—he'd just acquired a whole bunch of free fertilizer and wanted to know if she wanted some. At that time my wife was an avid gardener, and she was so thrilled she did a "happy dance" right there in the kitchen. When James showed up a few hours later with a load of manure, Jenni couldn't stop smiling and made her appreciation well known. My friend was the hero of the day. How could I have known a pickup bed full of composted cow dung was the key to her heart?

I could continue to make this a story about me and how lousy I am with gift giving, but really what I learned that Mother's Day, and continue to learn to this day, is how fascinating my wife is. Absolutely nothing about manure interests and excites me. Jenni, on the other hand, had been planning and working hard to create a gorgeous landscape and now saw a long-awaited opportunity to nurture flower beds and grow veggies. I admit there are times I throw my hands up in exasperated wonder, but I'm enthralled with the adventure of getting to know her. Learning more all the time keeps me interested and motivated; my constant learning makes her feel loved and cared for. I wouldn't have it any other way.

In chapter 3 we discussed fascination as the essence of romance. We talked about how curiosity comes naturally for children and how we can allow our curiosity to keep romance alive throughout our lives. We've even shown how our curiosity motivates us to explore and leads us to discovery. Underlying the journey to fascination is one foundational skill, one that's frequently underdeveloped and overlooked, but that when mastered, has the ability to vitalize a relationship. This skill is so basic it can be acquired by virtually anyone. It's the only skill that led me to more fully appreciate manure.

Discovering the "Quest" in Questions

There are no foolish questions, and no man becomes
a fool until he has stopped asking questions.
—Charles Proteus Steinmetz

What's the hidden secret to a life of fascination and discovery—of the world and each other? Believe it or not, a primary skill of all relational artists is simply *learning to formulate and ask great questions.* Inquiry forms the foundational building blocks for great relationships. At the helm of crusade and at the heart of romance, questions are central to feeling alive. Whether or not we're aware of it, the search for answers underlies all curiosity.

When my son Chris was pulling himself up to the bookshelf and grabbing hold of the plant, as I mentioned earlier, challenge and the urge of the unknown were moving him forward, and a series of questions began taking shape in his mind. As he looked at the shelf I'm sure he was thinking, *What's up there?* He then pulled himself up and while fingering the potting soil thought, *I wonder how this would taste?* His whole mini-adventure, driven by the need to know, ended with a muddy boy discovering what all little boys eventually learn: Dirt can be awesome. My son had encountered the "quest" in questions.

As Chris grew up he developed an interest in computers. His mom and I never have figured out how or from where this alien fascination emerged, but he became more and more intrigued. He'd ask us to take him to the library to check out computer textbooks he'd read for fun. I thought it was a bit strange, and I admit to having worried some about this odd child we'd birthed, but Chris's mind became filled with questions that drove him toward finding answers. Those answers spurred new inquiries, which propelled his interest and allowed his passion for computers to grow. Today he has his own Internet and Web design business. His skill and knowledge are so remarkable that when I'm tormented with technical difficulties, I thank God and call Chris.

Unfortunately, our world today doesn't usually recognize the value of questions; we don't encourage them or reward people for asking them. As a result, our society is made up of people trying to escape the boredom that results from not having a yearning to spur them on. As a former college professor, I'm convinced that one of our educational system's greatest disappointments is that we're feeding our children answers to questions they haven't yet asked. When the primary purpose of teaching becomes focused on the memorization of answers so kids can "get ahead in life" and make more money, the point of learning is lost.

The adventure in striving and searching is what drives the joy and excitement of learning. Similarly, we bump into the thrill of romance when we become infatuated by the unknown, but if we don't understand how curiosity fuels our fascination, romance fades. We succumb to the illusion of having run out of things to discover.

Overall, questions are even more important to me than answers. My need to discern and understand keeps me engaged; the more interesting the query, the more interesting the voyage, and the more satisfying the answer. Also, more carefully asked questions lead to more interesting information, which always has a huge bearing on the answers we get.

We must begin to get clear about what we really want to know. For instance, "Why am I so lousy at giving and receiving gifts?" is a good question. However, wanting to know what it is about manure that excites my wife brings about another result entirely. The focus of the two questions is markedly different; one is centered on me, the other on Jenni. Both could yield useful information, but they will most definitely take me on divergent paths.

The Advance of Great Relationships

Have you ever considered how most of the significant advances we enjoy in our world today have resulted from the works of inquiring minds? The quest for knowledge drives the process of exploration. Whether for Copernicus, discovering that the earth revolves around the sun, for Edison, designing a light bulb, or for you, figuring out how to save on your electric bill, a recognized need is the genesis of exploration. If you want to figure out how to have a great marriage—one both you and your spouse love—nothing will help you make more progress faster and more successfully than coming up with and asking great questions.

In the initial stages of new love, sharing is easy because we know so little about each other. At first everything is alive and interesting; the whole process seems brilliant. You both get to enjoy the journey of discovering a person who fascinates you, and you both get to enjoy being fascinating.

When Jenni and I first met at Humboldt State University (Trip to College #2), I was a student during the day and a musician at night. I'd spotted her in psych class the first day but hadn't yet paid much attention. After the second class, walking down the stairs behind me, she overheard a conversation I was having about my band playing that weekend at a local hot spot. Having only caught the part about my working at the club, she ascertained that I must be a bouncer or something, so she boldly interrupted and asked if I could get her in for free. Without much thought, I said I'd have her added to the guest list. That night she was surprised to find I was in the band, not working the door; she and her girlfriend stayed a little while, then left. I was focused on the performance so I didn't make much of it at the time.

The next day at school was cool and rainy. Etched into my memory like a movie scene in slow motion, the music stopped, and into class she sauntered: 5' 9", blond, blue eyes, complete with cowboy hat and boots. This city boy was about as far from "cowboy" as you could get, but my curiosity was piqued. I didn't remember much of the lecture because I knew that after class I was going to ask her out.

Trying my best to look nonchalant, I asked if she'd like to go to the campus coffee shop. By the time we arrived we were deep in conversation. I found her surprisingly interesting and easy to interact with. I kept learning things about her that would catch me off guard, which led me to ask more questions. She seemed genuinely surprised and interested in me too.

Eight hours later, the chairs were stacked upside down on the tables, the staff had swept around us twice, and we'd each made a first run through our life stories. Since we hadn't gotten the hint about closing time, finally we were politely asked to leave. After walking back to her car, we stood in the rain until saying our good-byes . . . and, of course, only after arranging our next rendezvous.

With time, not only have we learned lots of fun and endearing things about our mates, we've begun to find the flaws, blemishes, shortcomings, idiosyncrasies, and irritating habits. "Happily ever after" gets bumped out of the way while taking out the trash, doing the dishes, and wondering why we never get anywhere on time. Entering the picture is a whole host of factors that cause distractions and can play into shutting down the learning process. We'll address some of these shortly.

Remember, curiosity is a decision. To keep the flame burning brightly, we must continue pressing on toward new adventures in knowing and being known. Curiosity inspires the quest, and questions birthed out of wonder are the tools that animate the journey. Each of us can become a skilled investigator!

Let me implement a few questions myself to get us launched.

- *"Have you ever previously thought about how important intrigue is in keeping your romance alive?"* Most people I know have never thought this through. You've probably been caught up in dialogue with a wonderful conversationalist, but perhaps you've never taken time to notice that what makes them so engaging is how expertly they handle and ask questions. Or, maybe you're a good conversationalist but haven't realized how essential it is for you to use those skills continually in your marriage. Maybe you run out of things to ask and don't know what to do next. What-ever the case, the first step forward is recognizing that this skill is fundamental to an ongoing marital adventure and romance.
- *"Are you willing to become a student of the art of curiosity?"* Choosing to take the time and energy needed to invest in

mastering any new skill is challenging. It requires a willingness to become a student and face the awkwardness of both not knowing what you're doing and often fumbling while figuring it out. Acquiring most new skills involves a process of trial and error. We typically don't mind the "trial" part, but most of us hate the "error."

- *"Do you know how to formulate and ask questions that specifically build and deepen relationships?"* We all know how to retrieve information. "What's for dinner?" will draw a response but won't grow your relationship. Embracing the necessity of improving your art of curiosity is essential to ultimate success without making the journey sheer misery.

- *"How bad do you want it?"* This question goes a step beyond willingness to the point of desire. Being willing to go through whatever you must in order to become competent in a skill is important. However, seeing the potential rewards for your efforts and hungering for the end result is what will bring the motivation and stamina to persevere through to success.

When my children were little, each would go to the piano and want to play for us "a song they wrote." Of course, they didn't really know how to play, but they didn't yet know that. Their idea of music was passionate pounding on the keys while holding down the sustain pedal to make it extra special. Though we applauded their cuteness, the time came when each one had to realize he or she had no hope of ever becoming a pianist until first recognizing not knowing how to play. Only then could they put themselves in a position to learn.

I've gone through this same process in developing the art of asking great questions. I went into my marriage believing I had all I needed to be a fantastic husband. After bombing miserably, I finally accepted that there were relational skills and disciplines I didn't even know existed; "relationship-building questions" was among them. My desire kept me in the game, struggling to figure out and learn what I needed to learn until I succeeded. My desire has led me to seek until I find new ideas, and though I'm getting more skilled, my lessons haven't come without periodic rough patches.

Joe Romance

At one point in our marriage I became exasperated because no matter how hard I tried to communicate my affection for Jenni, I failed. I loved her and what I wanted most was to be her romantic hero. She made it clear that she was experiencing entirely the opposite. I thought the problem could be me, but if I loved her and regularly attempted to show it, I figured maybe it was her. Was she just impossible to please?

My internal debate haunted me enough that one day I was determined to solve it once and for all. All the way home from work I plotted and planned how I was going to sweep her off her feet and share my *amour* so powerfully it would weaken her knees. I was Joe Romance; she wouldn't be able to resist my charm.

I arrived home, put all my stuff down in the foyer, and waltzed into the kitchen where I found Jenni busy making dinner. Here was my chance. In an instant I smoothly swept in, whisked her off her feet, swung her around, and gave her a deep and passionate kiss. Pretty cool, huh? Well, she instantly got pretty hot with me, but unfortunately it wasn't the kind of heat I was hoping for. She was furious!

That cinched it; she *was* impossible. Here I was being every woman's dream and it still wasn't enough. I made a hasty exit and went off to nurse my bruised ego. As I left I had this nagging thought that I might still be missing something. I was frustrated *and* confused.

Wisely, I waited until after eating and tucking in the kids before asking what had gone wrong. Jenni was relaxing at the table with a cup of tea; I saw my chance. I sat down with her and said, "You know, I'm disappointed about the way things went when I got home tonight. I just wanted to let you know how much I love you, but clearly that didn't happen. What was it that made you upset?"

She paused, looked straight at me, and slowly, seriously asked, "Do you really want to know?"

Something in the way she inquired sent a momentary shiver (and brief second thoughts) through me, but, boy, was I frustrated, so I overcame the urge to run and said that, yeah, I really wanted to know. She proceeded to explain that at the moment I'd entered the kitchen she was simultaneously juggling ten things: trying to make dinner, keeping an eye on all four kids, minding the dogs, reaching for the phone.... My charging in and grabbing her felt reckless and selfish, as if I didn't care at all about *her;* like I wanted her to drop everything she was handling and just focus on me, as though nothing else in the world mattered. She felt completely *unloved.*

I could have argued or sulked, insisting that she'd gotten it all wrong, but in that instant I saw an opportunity to gain important insight into how I could more effectively transmit love from my heart into hers while showing her how much she means to me. The love was already there, but being her romantic hero requires me to share it in a way that warms her heart too. So I asked her this question: "Is there something I could have done differently that would have made you feel loved?"

She nodded. "As a matter of fact I can think of two things. If when you got to the kitchen you'd first paused to notice what was going on with me and how busy I was, that would have been a great start. Then if you'd have noticed the dishes piling up in the sink and started washing them, or even just asked me if there was anything you could do to help, I would have felt loved."

Not a storybook-fantasy depiction of a romantic hero, and not at all what I was expecting, but I must say, suddenly romancing my wife didn't seem nearly as daunting. Perhaps there was hope after all. I could do this; maybe this wasn't rocket science. Still, something else had me perplexed. Jenni had also seemed to react with marked disdain to the kiss. So I asked, "And, by the way, what was it about that kiss that upset you?"

Again she replied, "Do you really want to know?"

"Yes!"

She took a deep breath, as if this wasn't the first time she'd tried to communicate this. She explained that certain types of affection feel sexual and are very private to her; she becomes embarrassed when I give them in public. I think she may have used the word "grope." This had me stymied, because I feel totally different about it. In fact, I'd frequently attempted to honor her by doing my Tarzan routine, pounding my chest and showing the world how much I love *my woman*! But for heaven's sake, this time we were in our own kitchen.

"Bob, we were in front of the kids."

But you're my wife. This is my house. This is healthy.

It didn't matter what I thought. The possibility of being seen this way by the kids was embarrassing for her, and this discussion was to learn about her. And besides, I don't have to feel the same as her in order to care about her feelings. Remembering my goal of figuring out what made *her* actually feel loved, rather than what *I* wanted it to be, I asked her what I could have done that she would have appreciated and enjoyed.

"If you approached me like you do the girls, with gentle affection—a tender kiss, or wrapping your arms around my waist . . . or smoothing my hair back away from my face while asking about my day . . . but mostly offering to help shows me you really care about me . . . Besides, I think a man with his sleeves rolled up in the kitchen is sexy."

I thought, *I can do that.*

I got so excited about these breakthroughs, and the possibility of finally being her knight in shining armor, that I ran and got pen and paper. I know I'm a bit of a fanatic, but I wanted to get it right. I drew a line down the center of the page, creating two columns. The top of the first column was labeled, "Things that make Jenni feel loved." The second was labeled, "Things that make Jenni feel unloved." Then I began quizzing Jenni, filling in the information I wanted and needed.

What you must understand is that this story wasn't a onetime deal. I'm not the innocent party. Jenni's fury was in response to a long-standing pattern of physical insensitivities—repeated offenses of touching, tickling, and pinching. Men, here's a freebie: Women hate having their body space violated, even when it's well intended and when we'd never consider it invasive. Let her tease and invite you in.

My wife remains a mystery in many ways, and I'm still pursuing my post-doctorate in Jenni Paul. I've learned volumes over the years because I make it a priority to know and please her. The more I know her, the more intrigued I become. Sometimes I ask the questions out loud for her to answer, but many times my entreaties remain unspoken and I just pay close attention. One thing I know for sure: At this stage of life, my wife feels deeply loved by me. And whether it's a skillfully applied kiss or a pickup truck full of cow poop, well-thought-out questions helped me get here.

Tips for Creating Intrigue

The skill of formulating and asking great relational questions is imperative to finding your Ever After. Please keep in mind that the following suggestions are less a science than an art. Rather than approaching life with a formula, we must think of an intimate dance where we learn to move together in rhythm. Obviously, the more you intentionally practice using questions, the more graceful you'll become in the art. Your understanding and application of intrigue will become easier and easier. As time goes by, you'll also find it fun and satisfying.

Tip #1: Allow Your Curiosity to Create Questions

When a person is genuinely captivated by the learning process, questions naturally emerge one after another. Questions like, "I wonder if. . . ?" or "I wonder how. . . ?" or "I wonder why. . . ?" continue to flow. We allow our minds to move into a "figuring out" mode. Your spouse is a wealth of unique qualities, feelings, opinions, desires, and experiences. You can allow all of them to be a royal pain in the hindquarters, or you can see them as pieces of an amazing patchwork in God's design that intersects with yours. You may not like or agree with his or her unique personality and personal choices, but these have the possibility of being interesting, if we choose.

Tip #2: Embrace Confusion

My next advice for your quest toward intrigue: Welcome and embrace confusion. This may sound crazy, but I've come to appreciate life's ambiguity as one of my best friends and an almost endless source of great relational questions. Unfortunately, many people are afraid of turmoil or simply prefer to avoid uncomfortable feelings of uncertainty. However, I can guarantee the power of inquiry in your life and marriage; confusion is the ideal setting for revealing questions begging to be asked!

This principle has become one of the most powerful tools I use as a therapist. When a client is talking, I pay close attention, but especially so when he or she is saying something that doesn't *fully* make sense. I try to avoid making assumptions and filling in the blanks; instead, I stop and let the client know I'm not understanding or following what's being said or its meaning. My clients don't think I'm an idiot because I didn't understand plain English—most feel deeply cared for because I take extra time and care to make sure I understand their thoughts and *feelings* more clearly. This tool works as well, if not better, in your personal relationships. People are complex beings filled with apparent contradictions! We only must *want* to learn.

Imagine the consequence of seeing confusion as an asset to your relationship. Instead of withdrawal and judgment, I try responding to confusion with intrigue: "Tell me more, because I really want to get this; it seems important to understanding you." Or, "You're an amazing person. I never considered before now what you're saying, and I must confess I'm confused about what it all may mean." When an atmosphere of safety and caring is in place, confusion can actually be a doorway to comprehension. Rather than being destructive, this can be exhilarating. Herein confusion is not a threat but rather a signal that we're on the threshold of discovery.

Tip #3: See the Value of Unanswered Questions

I once had a graduate school professor point out that people tend to be in a continual process of explaining themselves to themselves, and that we're happiest when we have answers. We do this with many areas of life. Many of us become uncomfortable with questions lacking an immediate answer; we're left feeling undone.

However, we must realize that a measure of uncertainty brings us right to the heart of faith. I occasionally hear people criticize Christians, or believers of all faiths, for that matter, as weak-minded people who run to religion to avoid facing a world filled with uncertainty. Whereas this may be true for some, at the very foundation of our Christ-centered faith is a measure of believing without seeing—*of course* we have unanswered questions. If all we wondered about was explained, there would no longer be any mystery to God. Learning to live in the unanswered—that which you don't yet know and understand—is critical to opening your heart and mind to the beauty of mystery.

Tip #4: Make Use of Empathy

Empathy is attempting to put yourself in another's shoes; to see the world as someone else sees it and to feel what they're feeling. Don't confuse empathy with sympathy. Sympathy involves feeling sorry for someone and his circumstances. In contrast, the empathetic goal of seeing through another's eyes is not to determine what you would do in their situation but to deeply understand their unique viewpoint because you care about *them*.

Empathy is powerfully communicated through the type of questions you ask in your attempts to understand. As you delve into another's world, you will naturally encounter questions that must be asked and answered in order for you to fully understand, and for the other person to know that you do. The opportunities to do this in marriage are endless, but they're rarely seized. Taking time to ask questions communicates genuine care and love.

Relationship Questions

Never be afraid to ask the question, especially of yourself.
Discovery is the mission of life.
— Brian Kates

Questions are so powerful in building great relationships that even God loves them. Questions show that we are interested and that we care enough to ask:

> Ask and it will be given to you; seek and you will find;
> knock and the door will be opened to you. For everyone

who asks receives; he who seeks finds; and to him who
knocks, the door will be opened. (Matthew 7:7–8)

God encourages us to have the heart of a seeker. King David was
revered as the ultimate seeker, a man after God's own heart (Acts
13:22). The intimate inquiry toward knowing and being known
defines a great relationship question.

Carefully posed questions focus on discovery and steer away
from judgment or agendas. Therefore, it helps to ask yourself first
why you're asking. How to ask great questions without sounding
like a detective or a prosecutor? The answer is found in asking
yourself:

*Am I motivated by a quest to understand and care, versus
any other agenda?*

Human beings have an uncanny ability to sense insincerity, judgment, and manipulation, and we have a natural inclination to avoid
all three. When the overarching goal is first to care and then to
understand, even poorly formed conversation may still be effective
because everybody stays relaxed. Without a context of caring and
safety, no question will be productive to the relationship; instead, it
will be viewed with suspicion and resistance. The intent behind the
inquiry has enormous bearing on how it will be received and how
useful it will be toward building the relationship.

Relationship building is not an interrogation. Make sure the
search itself does not set the agenda or direction of the conversation, or you will likely encounter a hesitant or unwilling partner.
Remember: If you're probing into the inner world of your spouse's
thoughts and feelings, you are literally treading into sacred territory—inside the "temple of the Holy Spirit" (1 Corinthians 3:16;
6:19). The information contained within is precious, valuable, and
vulnerable. Consider your entry not as an entitlement, but a privi-

lege given by invitation. Questions are helpful in promoting an atmosphere of caring and safety when they give control to the responder for what's discussed, when it's discussed, and how it's discussed.

Consider some of the following examples:

- "What would you like me to understand about you and your heart on this issue?"
- "What are you feeling?"
- "Where would you like our focus to be?"
- "What do you want?"
- "What do you think would be best here?"

Such questions express interest, concern, and curiosity but let the responder regulate how vulnerable she is with the response. In this way the inquirer is assuming a position of curiosity without judgment or control of where the conversation goes. If the inquest's goal is to judge or find fault rather than to care and understand, people feel suspicious and unsafe. Interrogation posed with the intent to trap normally isn't hard to recognize. We seem to instinctively know when a question is posed for the purpose of discovery versus to gain advantage in a conflict. It is easier to recognize bad dialogue than good.

Unproductive questions are often focused on blame and establishing facts. When it comes to being curious and discovering my own heart, and my partner's, we've found four ways to ask that are generally *not* helpful.

(1) Who is right, and who is wrong?
(2) Who is at fault or who's to blame?
(3) What really happened?
(4) What should we do to fix this problem?

These question-tracks lead us away from curiosity and understanding; they pull us toward judgment and problem-solving.

Judgment, more often than not, is a complete waste of time that causes people to feel unsafe, to want to retreat and close up. Problem-solving can obviously play a useful part in great relationships, but timing is everything; problem-solving can shift the focus from the heart to the head without first connecting at an emotional level. The energy is wasted if we don't believe the other cares about what we feel, think, or want.

Many times the important questions don't even need to be voiced. *What is she really feeling right now?* may not need to be spoken but rather allowed to direct your attention, concern, and behavior. When internal questions are asked for the purpose of caring about and understanding your spouse, and ultimately growing a better marriage, compassion will likely constrain you from moving too quickly to express your own feelings before you really grasp, and allow yourself to be impacted by, your spouse's concerns. With all of this going on inside, your spouse may not even realize you've asked the question, but I guarantee he or she will feel it over time (if not immediately). It is a genuine expression of love.

Conclusion

Whether standing in awe and wonder while gazing up at the night sky, or seeking to understand why your wife is upset when she arrives home, I believe you will find the quest itself to be the Holy Grail. Rather than seeking to change each other, I hope you will pause and discover anew the depth of intrigue within the heart of your loved one. The way in which we pose our questions speaks volumes about our love and concern.

Ask great questions. It's an art form worthy of mastery.

─────────── *to* Ponder *and* Discuss ───────────

1. What kinds of things in life keep you interested and curious?

2. What do you think about the idea of developing the art of curiosity

and learning to formulate and ask great questions?

3. Have you allowed yourself to remain curious about your spouse and actively engaged in getting to know him/her more deeply? If not, what keeps you from doing so?

4. In what ways can you see using confusion as a source of questions to grow and deepen your marriage? In other words, when you're confused, turn your lack of understanding into understanding by asking questions.

5. How do you generally feel when someone asks you questions about yourself—guarded, uneasy, or cared for? How much does your trust in the person and the motive behind the question make a difference?

6. What makes you feel loved? What makes your spouse feel loved?

7. If probing into the inner world of your spouse is literally treading into sacred territory, how does this change the way you approach him/her?

CHAPTER 8

— REVEAL —
The Joy of Discovery

Words are just words, and without heart
they have no meaning.
—Chinese Proverb

One day, Chris, then four, walked up to me and, with the seriousness of a twenty-year-old, asked, "Dad, can we talk?"

I was so taken by surprise that for a brief moment I didn't know how to respond. This had all the makings of the "twilight zone," and I expected to start hearing that eerie music playing in the background. More than a little amused, I couldn't wait to see where this was going; I looked down at the little boy whose head barely came past my knees, and I nodded. "Sure, son."

We walked over to the couch and sat down together for our first serious father-son chat. Without missing a beat he looked at me and asked, "So, how ya doin'?"

163

I almost couldn't contain the smile threatening to blow my cover. I paused for an appropriate second of reflection and replied, "Pretty good . . . how about you?"

He said, "Pretty good too."

We sat for a moment in silence. Finally Chris spoke up and asked, "So, how ya doin'?"

We went through the appropriate social graces a couple more times, and then I concluded with a handshake. "It's been great talking with you. Let's do it again soon."

With that he hopped down off the couch and ran outside to play in the sandbox.

My son had obviously been observing the adults around him and had begun to notice patterns in how we typically communicate; in particular, how we start conversations. What he hadn't yet figured out was how to move beyond a cordial greeting and opening line. I think a lot of us can relate to the awkward space of wanting to move on in dialogue when we get that feeling of being stuck without clear direction. Our hands get clammy; we look for the nearest exit.

Especially when it comes to intimate communication, many of us are just like four-year-old Chris. We know the basics of how to get started, but we quickly come to the end of our knowledge and skill. Once the conversation moves toward deeper levels of uncharted territory and lurking areas of vulnerability, we're mired. We come to a critical point where the potential risk seems to outweigh the possible gain, and we simply don't know how to successfully traverse rough spots in the terrain.

We don't need to carry all the weight of navigating the trek alone. Conversation always involves at least two traveling partners. We can enjoy the process. We don't have to be so cerebral in our journey to discovery. An awe-inspiring romance begins when our head meets our own heart—a combination of understanding and caring. It then finds its completion when our heart opens and connects with another.

With the foundational skill of exploration through asking great questions, we can now press on toward the joy of discovery: intimacy. In marriage, two eternal beings are united for a brief moment on this earth to learn about one another, about life together, and about walking with God. Revelation of the heart brings striking disclosure. With disclosure passion ignites. And when the flames are safely contained, a marriage adventure is filled with warmth and excitement.

I laugh at scenes depicting two lovers who just happened to arrive at the same place at the same moment and within minutes are mad with passion. Across the crowded subway station, his eyes meet hers and all is revealed—bingo! They're soul mates; love prevails.

Doesn't seem to happen that way in real life. Instead, he didn't hear what she was trying to say, and she got angry when he asked, "What *is* your problem?" He tries to please her and she doesn't get it . . . you know how it is, we have real-life fumbling going on when it comes to sharing our intimate selves.

What lies ahead separates the heroes from the "extras" on life's movie set. We must be ready and willing, as they used to say on *Star Trek*, "to boldly go where no man has gone before." We've not only been assigned our own stunt work, we're doing the love scenes too! So *how* do we gracefully reveal our soul to the one we adore?

The number one problem reported by couples when they come to us for counseling is communication. This is such a common source of relational frustration, it's not likely to come as a surprise. What is surprising? That we've known about this for ages and don't seem to be making much headway.

Many of us have invested a lot in reading and training for effective communication, yet isn't it remarkable how often the same successful businesspeople that have been professionally trained in effective interpersonal skills do not recognize how those same skills apply to their marriage? The communication tools that are landing the big deals at work could also score big at home. For many couples the information has been available but they've never heard it, at least not in a manner they could understand and practically put to use with their loved ones. This is clearly an area in which information alone is not sufficient to inspire change. Toward that end, let me share with you the most basic, up-to-date form of intimate communication I know.

Simpler Is Always Better!

Simplicity is the ultimate sophistication.
—Leonardo da Vinci

I hold tightly to a philosophy, especially when it comes to talking with my wife: "Simpler is always better!" There's no better place to put this mission into practice than in sensitive dialogue. One of the primary spots in which people get stuck and spin out begins with the assumption that communication between two people who speak the same language *should* be easy. The truth: Verbal communication is so complex that being able to understand the words another person is saying, and then being able to comprehend what they mean, is nothing short of amazing! *Mis*understanding is far more likely to happen. Instead of getting frustrated and angry with each other when misunderstood, we should be enthusiastically congratulating and exchanging high-fives when we do understand! So by first acknowledging that verbal communication is complex, we're off to a good start on simplifying it. Let me explain.

Look at the symbol below. What do you see?

Your most likely response is the letter A. Why—why the letter A instead of just three intersecting lines? Most of us answer that someone (Big Bird?) told us it's the letter A. The broader answer is that somewhere in history this symbol came to represent a building block of our language. It was given a name and assigned a corresponding sound or series of sounds, and it follows a set of rules. As far as we know this wasn't God-ordained, because billions around the globe use different language systems.

When Chris was learning to read, he'd get very frustrated with some of what we were trying to teach him. Independently minded from birth, he regularly had his own ideas about how things should be. One day, while I was working with him on the alphabet, he threw himself down on the floor and had a full-blown tantrum over a letter that he thought should have a different name and sound. I finally threw my hands up and exclaimed, "Chris, I swear I had nothing to do with this. It was decided long before either of us got here."

The point is, every time we look at a symbol, we go through an amazing process of interpretation. Most of us don't really remember how hard it was to learn to read, and now we've been doing it so long we take it for granted. We look at a series of letters strung together to make a word, like D-O-G. What does it mean? Most people think of a furry, four-legged animal. But what if we were playing basketball, and when you drove right past me to score I said, "You dog!" Am I calling you a furry, four-legged animal? No, I'm expressing my disdain for being shown up on the court—and you'd know it as soon as I said it.

Listening for Heaven's Sake, a wonderful book on communication, cites a researcher from UCLA who suggests that only 7 percent of the meaning we get from verbal communication comes from the words themselves. He claims the other 93 percent comes from the nonverbal cues like tone of voice, body language, and context. His point is driven home by the following exercise: Repeat this sentence of the same six words one sentence at a time, making sure to emphasize the different bolded and italicized word each time.

I didn't say you were stupid.

I didn't *say* you were stupid.

I didn't say *you* were stupid.

I didn't say you *were* stupid.

I didn't say you were **stupid.**

Notice that the same words said in the same order mean something different each time just by changing which word is stressed. We're usually able to figure out the message, but we must keep in mind how subjective this exchange of information can be.[1]

If you keep this in mind when trying to communicate, and therefore extend patience and grace rather than intolerance and frustration, you've already set yourself up to make the process easier. Furthermore, you've greatly increased the likelihood of successfully sending a message that's understood by the listener to mean what you intended. One of my colleagues, Dr. Robert Burbee, suggests from his experience that approximately 75 percent of marital conflict is due to simple misunderstanding. If this is true, we should be able to easily eliminate the majority of what stumps us just by this step alone.

In this chapter we'll discuss a communication method that can be a powerful tool for couples to begin the process of discovery with each other. Bear in mind: The real catalyst for changing relationships is most likely not the skill of articulating words, but the environment in which two people feel safe enough together to open up and reveal their true selves.

As already discussed, openhearted and free with one another is how we were created to be. Even now most of us would acknowledge that when we feel safe in a relationship, being vulnerable about ourselves or being curious about the other person doesn't require much effort. Unfortunately, life experience has taught us not to trust others or to be open to their perspective and experience. It may take considerable effort to *establish* safety and *maintain* it well enough to remain open.

The skill of making ourselves known is a tool to establish safe and open communication and to keep the exchange uninhibited once it's begun. Have you ever had the opportunity to carefully examine what safe communication can look like and how to make it happen? Let's first consider two very different relating styles that seem to be present in relationships with great communication. When we consider couples who appear to articulate themselves easily and freely, we see at least two types of talking taking place.

Work Talk

The first style I refer to as "Work Talk," which tends to be a linear way of sharing information. When we need to discuss getting a task accomplished, we typically use Work Talk. If Jenni and I are figuring out who's taking Nathan to soccer practice or how to deal with a problem at the office, we need a form of communication that will best enable us to complete the task at hand. The goal of Work Talk is to be productive and efficient.

The Work Talk focus is not on sharing feelings. Even if emotion does get mixed in, the primary goal is not intimacy. The goal is to weigh alternatives, select the best, and move on to the next issue. The conversation is carried by what seems most logical and sensible to solving a problem or planning an event; it's important for a couple to have the ability to utilize Work Talk when it's needed. Done well, this style of imparting information results in a win for the team.

Heart Talk

A second style of open and candid communicators is about disclosing information in a much more relational way. We refer to this as "Heart Talk" because it's more about hearts connecting than about proficiency or achievement. Heart Talk pursues understanding while allowing for an exploration of an issue's depth and breadth.

Marriage is fundamentally about love and desire, both of which are matters of the heart. Intimacy too is about sharing who we are in increasing depth, including our feelings, secrets, dreams, etc., which are also heart matters. Therefore, the primary communication type we'll address here is Heart Talk, which involves pulling in close, seeking to understand and care for each other. Usually more focused on the people involved than the task at hand, Heart Talk frequently includes thinking through nuances and subtleties of an issue, as well as some type of exploration involving curiosity. Such disclosure allows couples to feel deeply understood, to share a sense of belonging together.

A good analogy for Heart Talk can be found in dancing. When two people dance for fun and not for competition, they may have an idea of the steps they're going to follow, but the experience of moving as one is what counts, not getting to the other side of the room. Their rhythm and flow is not pursued for the purpose of completing a task. People generally dance because they enjoy experiencing the music and movement together. Another analogy is two friends getting together for lunch as an opportunity to catch up. After an hour they part company, grateful for their time together— they met no particular agenda, but they feel more closely connected.

Getting to the Heart of the Matter

One learns people through the heart, not the eyes or the intellect.
— Mark Twain

My friend Kris and his wife, Leslye, had two older boys when a beautiful, surprise package arrived. They were all overjoyed, but life wasn't going to be easy for Baby Claire. She was born with challenging health issues, and as time went on they discovered she has a fairly severe seizure disorder. It was during the search for a diagnosis that this part of Kris's story unfolds.

By the time Claire was just three years old, she'd already endured many frightening and painful tests before having to make a trip to the cardiologist for still more tests. She lives in a house with big guys, and she's our little princess. She's timid anyway, and she was scared to death while the doctors were poking and prodding her. This day they did four or five more major tests. They had just finished doing an EKG, when they started a procedure I'd never seen before. My dad had heart trouble so I'm familiar with many of the tests, but nothing like this.

The docs wanted to take a picture of her heart on a 3D imaging system. All my nerves were on high alert, feeling defensive for my little princess, who was scared out of her wits. Still, at the same time I'm thinking as she's lying there, *Do you have any idea how much this is going to cost me?* Then my thoughts would take the other side, *But she's worth it. . . .*

The doctor calmly explained that he was going to take her shirt off, that her mommy and daddy were going to be right there holding her hand. Quietly he said his nurse was going to squirt some cold lotion on her chest. The nurse started rubbing the goo around, and as the doctor told Claire that see, it doesn't hurt at all, she started freaking out, kicking and screaming, "No! No!" I too tried to get close enough where I could look her in the eyes and convince her it wasn't going to hurt, and what the doctor was doing was a good thing, but she just kept fighting.

She had to be absolutely still to pull this off. I felt the urgency of the test, but even more I wanted to comfort my baby. Finally, I climbed up on the table and cradled her in my arms. Only then did she stop crying and begin to relax. The doctor explained what he was going to do, and he began moving the instrument around her chest.

When my wife was pregnant with my boys, we had caveman technology. Sonograms back then gave a little blip and the technician would point out the eyes and nose. I hear they now take a Polaroid, but back then it was like, "Oh, look at the little hand," and I'd say, "Right. I see that!" Well, this test was nothing like that. I'd never seen anything quite this high-tech. The doctor moved the instrument and into clear view I saw a chamber of Claire's heart. What appeared wasn't just a big blob; I could see every detail of her heart. Then he started explaining what he was looking for before he changed positions—calling the shots is what I call it. He'd say, "Now the blood that's flowing into her heart is going to be blue, while the blood flowing out of her heart is going to be red. Here's what I'm looking for," and at one point he showed us a tiny valve. "You're going to see this valve open and close, but watch this next valve carefully. When I get to it, it's going to leak a little bit so you'll see just a trace of blood coming back into her heart from that valve."

While he's showing us this stuff, I'm cradling my little princess in my arms and looking at her pulsing heart. Part of me is amazed by the technology. Because I'm a guy, I'm thinking that I gotta have one of those machines! No idea what I would do with it, but nobody else has one. The other part of me has my own heart beating out of my chest because I'm so aware that this is my baby. I looked down into her sweet face as she was snuggled down in my arms, and you know what? Cost was no longer even a consideration. Her heart is worth a billion dollars to me. While I was there watching it beat, my heart was thumping like it's never beat before. I was looking at hers reflected there on the screen and thinking, *How could anyone hurt this? Who would ever hurt this innocent, helpless little girl?*

After this astounding moment, Kris had an epiphany about the value of the human heart (both figuratively and physically). He said, "This is how we have to start seeing and treating each other's hearts, Bob! The people God gave us—they're our most precious gift in this life! I can imagine that if I could do a sonogram of my wife's heart, there are things written there that I couldn't just say, 'Well, get over it, hon!'"

Kris got a high-tech view of the heart, and as a result he's a changed man. He saw the value of Claire's heart, and his wife's heart is worth a billion dollars to him too.

"When it comes to matters of the heart, we are all just as helpless as my little Claire. We all need to be tended to with great care. I too need somebody to honor me."

Since Heart Talk deals with heart matters, it commonly involves areas of vulnerability. Heart Talk can be successfully engaged when the heart of each spouse is open and available. Each needs to be confident that his or her heart will be well tended and that the information shared will be handled with great care. If either person has any serious concern about paying a price for entering into the conversation, he/she will be reluctant to fully participate.

Back to the Work Talk/Heart Talk contrast for a moment. When provided with the explanation of these two styles, most people can identify quickly which style is their "default" way of processing an issue in relationships. Based on observation of couples who go through our Intensive programs, we estimate as many as 85 percent of the husbands are primarily Work Talkers. Women are not so easily described. As a group, women more regularly associate with the Heart Talk style, perhaps as many as 50 percent. However, another sizable group, approximately 25–30 percent, says they flip back and forth between styles depending on the circumstances.

In a relationship, it's not hard to see that if one person is in

Work Talk mode and the other is wanting Heart Talk, communication is likely to break down; nevertheless, we know that both styles are present in couples who clearly articulate. There's a preferred sequence to these styles in the couples we refer to as having great communication: They show a preference to beginning with Heart Talk before taking on the task at hand with Work Talk. It seems these couples attempt to build a solid foundation of understanding and care first, and then make the shift to problem-solving or formulating strategy. It is interesting to note how often a conflict is resolved through Heart Talk without the necessity of Work Talk. Sometimes conflicts that appear on the surface to require a decision are resolved without any decision-making at all, through a profound connection of the heart. If Heart Talk has this degree of power to resolve conflict and promote relationship, then doing it well is a valuable marriage-relationship skill.

Heart Talk: The ICU Model

We've seen that for individuals to feel safe enough to open their hearts to each other and enjoy sharing intimately, caring is the key. Nowhere are the benefits more evident, and the care more critical, than when entering into the vulnerable world of self-disclosure. In those moments you are each handling two priceless hearts. The more you care, the easier your relationship becomes and the more successful you will be. Toward that end we want to encourage you to consider making your marriage a relational "ICU," an intensive *care* unit. A hospital ICU is where patients receive the highest-level care available because of the gravity of their illness or injury. We would like you to create your marital ICU not so much because of the *need* to be cared for but more because of the *value* of those being cared for. There is no more effective way to facilitate meaningful and satisfying intimate communication.

Consider the impact of viewing your own heart and your

spouse's heart as deserving of all the precaution and attention of an ICU. Approaching Heart Talk as if you were entering the ICU creates a secure foundation for intimate dialogue: sensitive, alert, and attentive to safety at all times. Our Heart Talk method was created to help us safely approach intimacy, wherein we're invited to look into the soul of another. The ICU (I see you) model of Heart Talk is the simplest and most powerful way we know to get you there.

The beauty of ICU is that it's the first communication model I know of that requires both people—the speaker and the listener—to remember only the same three simple principles: I-C-U. We'll spend some time here discussing and elaborating on how to use Heart Talk and the ICU model, but when you're actually engaged in conversation, the only things you must remember to pull it off are: I-C-U.

I—"Identify" the feelings of the speaker.
C—"Care" about those feelings.
U—"Understand" those feelings.

We've found that when a person's heart is appropriately, sensitively, and consistently cared for and understood, faith in the other begins to be established. When a couple works together to make their marriage a safe haven, where trust becomes the norm in their everyday environment, they're able to relax. When two people become that confident and comfortable with each other, they naturally open up, and the world of intimate connection opens up with it.

One of the weaknesses that I find in most of today's communication methods is that success is generally dependent on the effort and skill of the listener. The ICU model of Heart Talk is designed to share the burden and responsibility equally between the speaker and the listener, which is where it belongs. Bridging the gap between us in order to transcend our separateness and truly connect, using words, requires a sender and a receiver; both must be present and active for the effort to be effective. As husband and wife we then join together in this intricate exercise, invested in carefully exploring each other's fascinating and vulnerable inner world of feelings, emotions, hopes, and desires. We become caring team-mates engaged in an ongoing enterprise of maintaining a relational ICU that encourages our hearts to soar and our love to flourish.

Remember also that successful communication starts by acknowledging that verbal discourse is complex and misunder-standing is common. For developing your understanding of and skill with the ICU model, let's discuss each of the three elements in more detail.

I: *Identify Feelings*

The first step for both speaker and listener is to identify the feelings of the speaker. When people communicate, a lot of information is exchanged. If we're talking about anything intimate or even remotely personal, emotions are always involved, which naturally creates a level of vulnerability. If, in addition, a hot button has been pushed during the exchange or there's been any hint of conflict, an onslaught of feelings enters the scene. Some sentiments may be obvious; others may remain hidden or unspoken.

Whether or not we know it, in that moment some level of fear has been triggered in one or both participants, and all the natural fight or flight mechanisms go on high alert. Affirming that impor-tant feelings are present is a powerful way of honoring those feel-ings, thus honoring the person having them. At this stage there doesn't need to be understanding or agreement of any kind. How-ever, recognizing how fully one's feelings are involved is extremely important. Identifying those feelings is the essential first step.

Why *start* with identifying feelings? The amazing pattern we've seen consistently over the years is that until people feel seen and heard emotionally, the conversation will stall. The person experiencing the emotions often unconsciously attempts to deal with his or her own feelings and attempts to get the other person to do so as well. This may take the form of trying to control the other person, or getting them to hear your point or focus on you and your agenda. Sometimes it's by convincing the other person how wrong they are or how they've hurt you, embarrassed you, annoyed you, etc. There are countless ways this can go, but the most important point is that until you feel your feelings are seen and heard, your focus will tend to stay centered on you.

When two people in the same conversation are each focusing on themselves, the conversation begins a dizzying cycle of futility, frustration, and pain. Ultimately, each wants to have his or her own passions cared for and understood; the way to start breaking the cycle is to stop the madness and focus on *one person at a time.* In order to be able to effectively care for and understand one's feelings, we must first identify them.

The *I* in the ICU model means the speaker is to identify his or her own issues rather than what triggered them. The goal is *not* to get your spouse to do something about it. The speaker's first goal: Identify your emotions so *you* are aware of them. This is critical! If your underlying intent is to get your spouse to take responsibility for how you see things and to move to a better place emotionally, the conversation quickly turns to a form of manipulation and control; your goal is to get your spouse to do something different so you can experience something different. Manipulating or controlling your spouse is not at all helpful in Heart Talk; avoid it.

Here, in the process, increased awareness of yourself and your perceptions is extremely valuable. The more clearly you can identify *what* you are experiencing, the better off you will be. It's great to have Jenni really understand how I feel, but it's even better when I fully comprehend it first. I've come to realize that frequently I'm not nearly as clear about what's really going on with me as I think I am in the moment. Strong impressions often cloud my judgment.

I've also found that when strong emotions are present, multiple reactions frequently occur at the same time, sometimes even contradictory and conflicted feelings.

The listener's first goal: Identify what's going on within the heart of the speaker. The speaker may or may not be clear on his or her own feelings, but regardless, you need to enter into "curiosity, explore, and discover" mode. Your initial job is to reflect back to him/her what you think his or her feelings might be. It's okay to be wrong; this kind of communication is challenging for everyone. Just keep at it until you hear some version of "Yeah, that's it!"

You've succeeded in this step when the two of you are both clear about what feelings are present. Please remember that this exercise is entering the private world of the speaker, and, therefore, he or she always has the final say about what feelings are present. As the listener, *don't* say, "That's not what you're really feeling." Honor each other by always allowing the speaker to be the ultimate authority of his or her own heart.

C: *Caring*

Once identified, those feelings can be cared for . . . by both of you. Speaker: Simply decide that those elements are important because *you* are important *to you*. If this sounds odd, hang in there with me—it's a very important distinction. Most people mistakenly think that attending to your own sensitivity is shown by trying to get someone to care about how you feel. Trying to get someone to do anything is a form of manipulation. This is about *consideration,* not manipulation. So first extend care and compassion toward yourself.

If your attitude is "I hate these feelings and I want to get rid of them," or "I hate myself because I have these stupid reactions," there is no compassion in that. If you came across a person you loved who was hurting, what would make that person feel most supported: loving the person with the feelings or trying to get rid of the feelings? I promise that across the board, attending to the person and wrapping your arms around both the person and their feelings would bring about the most love.

Typically, the average person does not initially see that hating one's own sentiments seems very much like hating oneself. The goal is not to love the emotions; it's to care about the person having those emotions (you) and to at least welcome the truth about where you are in that moment. Don't worry if this sounds strange; I'm positive that once you begin to understand and put this into practice, you'll see a difference.

Then, from a place of being conscious of yourself and your own feelings, you can honor those feelings enough to be willing to share them with your spouse and ask him or her to stand by you also. When I ask Jenni to care about my emotions *with me*, it feels very different to her than when I ask her to care about them *for me*. My ability to feel cared for is not wholly dependent on what Jenni does or doesn't do with my heart.

When I have strong emotions going on, there's always a great likelihood that Jenni does too. As a mere mortal, there are times she's so caught up in dealing with her own inner struggle that it's hard to be able to care about my heart also. If she's not able to handle my heart carefully at that time, I have no business extending it out to her; it's too valuable and too vulnerable. Better to wait until she's ready, willing, and able. Of course, I can always start by listening to her heart first if *I'm* able at that time.

As the listener, my goal is to care about her, to allow her feelings to impact me and matter to me. I used to believe I couldn't respond appropriately to someone's deepest concerns unless I understood or agreed with them. I'm thankful to report I was wrong! I now see that I can accept another's feelings whether or not I understand or agree.

Typically, I know when Jenni is upset or hurt or anxious or afraid. I can care about those feelings because I love her. At that point, I don't need to understand why she's feeling what she is in order to attend to her; I only need to know that she's not happy about it. If she's even mildly irritated, I can be concerned about that too because I cherish her. (Note: this method works every bit as well with positive feelings, it's just that we don't have as many problems with those.)

Another problem I encountered while attempting to listen and care was an unconscious fear that responding to how someone felt would require me to do what they wanted me to do. This belief often made the decision to care feel like betraying myself. Internally I was in a bind, so I would unconsciously choose to stay focused on myself, which essentially is not caring about the other person. I'm so glad that caring for another does not require me to choose him or her over my own well-being.

For example, I can care about my wife and myself at the same time. Special regard for Jenni's feelings is not the same as doing what she wants me to do. If she's unhappy, that matters to me. However, my feelings matter too. For any situation to work out toward the betterment of our marriage, both of us must feel good about it; both sets of feelings need to matter. Remember, Jenni is my teammate, so I lean heavily on the no-losers policy.

U: *Understand*

Once I've identified the feelings and chosen to care for them, I now take the step of attempting to understand. The goal for both is to learn more about the speaker by seeking to better understand those emotions and where they're coming from. As already mentioned, I often think I have myself pretty well figured out when I begin to share with Jenni what I'm perceiving, only to discover all sorts of things going on in me that I didn't even realize. Therefore, I enter Heart Talk expecting to learn about myself through the process also. When I approach it this way rather than as if I'm going to teach Jenni about Bob, the resulting exploration into Bob's emotional world feels much more like an adventure and a romantic journey we're taking together. It has the potential to be an amazing ride that can draw people together in astounding ways.

For me as the listener, Jenni's emotions are not random or arbitrary. Understanding her heart helps me to better understand Jenni. Her emotions are a part of the fabric of who she is, and even though her passion often challenges me and triggers a bunch of my own feelings, I want her to know I'm trying to understand. In fact, I want to be a man who cares about people, especially about his wife. Heart Talk creates the ideal opportunity to walk into the heart's precious and sacred places safely, richly, and meaningfully, enabling us to fully appreciate the handiwork of an amazing God through the journey of knowing another person.

Steps for Heart Talk

(1) Either spouse can initiate Heart Talk anytime either or both are experiencing strong emotions (positive or negative). The initiating question could be as simple as "Would you be willing to have some Heart Talk on this topic?"

(2) Commit to creating a relational ICU (Intensive *Care* Unit).

(3) Determine who will begin as the speaker (remember, you will soon switch).

(4) Continue communication until the speaker feels understood, not when the listener thinks he or she understands.

(5) Switch roles once the initial speaker feels complete on that topic.

Speaker	Listener
I = Identify and talk about your feelings. • Focus on how you feel, *not* what he/she did or didn't do. (Avoid blame.)	**I = Identify and reflect back what your spouse is feeling.** • Focus on what he/she feels, *not* what your spouse claims you did or didn't do.
C = Care for your feelings. • Allow your feelings to matter to you; give your heart a voice. • Request and expect that your spouse also be careful.	**C = Care for your spouse's feelings.** • Communicate that you care: "How you feel matters to me because *you* matter to me." • Allow your spouse's feelings to touch your heart and impact you.
U = Seek to understand your own feelings better. • Be responsible with/for your feelings (my feelings, my responsibility). • Identify what "buttons" were pushed. • Explore your feelings and their origins more deeply.	**U = Seek to understand your spouse's feelings.** • Seek to understand what he/she is feeling, and why, without trying to "fix it." • Put yourself in his/her shoes (empathy). • Be curious/interested, non-judgmental, encouraging, and validating.

Helpful Hints

1. Ask for time. (Ask permission to share your feelings or hear your spouse's.)
2. Remember: Anytime a person is sharing his/her heart (emotions, feelings, etc.), that information is worthy of the highest honor,

respect, and care; it's private, sacred information.

3. Understand that caring for your own feelings does not necessarily equal:

- Resolving the issue.
- Making your feelings more important than your spouse's.
- Expecting your spouse to be responsible for your feelings (e.g., "You made me feel this way," or "I can't feel better unless you . . .")
- Telling yourself your feelings are wrong, bad, or stupid.
- Demanding that your spouse admit guilt or apologize.

4. Understand what caring for your mate's heart does not necessarily equal:

- Resolving the issue.
- Agreeing with what he/she says, how he/she feels, or "what really happened."
- Being responsible for his/her feelings or trying to "fix it."
- Making changes.
- Admitting guilt or apologizing.

5. As the listener, you can make a validating and caring statement before switching roles (e.g., "Thanks for sharing your feelings," or "That makes sense," or "You and your feelings really matter to me").

Validation: Brick-and-Mortar

Critical opportunity for the listener takes place at the moment of switching roles, which can dramatically deepen the heart connection. I like to think of this opportunity as applying mortar to the bricks of understanding: It is the opportunity for validation. Without it you could have a bunch of bricks stacked together but nothing truly binding them together. People skilled at validation are typically never at a loss for friends; people who validate others impart life and encouragement to everyone they meet. So what does it entail?

In its various forms, validation carries the message that *you are valuable to me*. The effort I expend in trying to *understand* your emotional message is validating to some degree, but a *confirming* statement will carry at least two elements.

First, it will convey, "You're not crazy for feeling that way." In other words, another sane person in the same shoes might feel the same thing.

Second, it will lend some expression of "It matters to me to know you feel this way." That is, "What I've heard is valuable information, and I care about what you've shared." Especially if my perspective is different from my spouse, validating her before I share my view demonstrates my commitment to her; it cements that I value her and our relationship more than the issue we're discussing.

Again, it's possible to validate while not necessarily agreeing or apologizing. I could begin my response with the following statement: "I can sure see how you might feel that way, and it makes sense to me. What you're feeling matters to me a great deal. I have a different perspective on this issue, if you're open to it."

The last statement is to double-check that my spouse is truly ready to hear my view. Out of respect for myself and for her, I don't want to move on unless I have a ready listener. This step usually leads to a more motivated listener, because she has now been heard and can give me her undivided attention.

Conclusion

Communication is tricky, but it doesn't have to be painful and disappointing. When two people commit to tending each other's concerns with the same care as would be received in the Intensive Care Unit, they're free to explore and care for their own hearts and respond in kind. Simpler is always better.

Are you a great communicator? Tap the efficiency of Work Talk, but give first priority to drawing near with Heart Talk. You'll find the ICU model extraordinary. Discover. Reveal. Enjoy.

———————— *to* Ponder *and* Discuss ————————

1. Do you prefer small talk or intimate conversation? Are you usually more comfortable with "Work Talk" or "Heart Talk"? Why?

2. Describe how it feels for you to get in touch with your own feelings. How do you usually handle your own feelings?

3. Describe how it feels for you to get in touch with how your spouse feels. How do you usually handle his/her feelings? Do you judge them—say they are wrong, stupid, wacky, selfish, over-sensitive—or do you value and welcome them?

4. Have you ever disclosed something that made you feel vulnerable and then had those feelings used against you? Has your spouse ever shared feelings that you later used against him/her?

5. What happens in conversation that helps you feel cared for and understood?

6. When you share your feelings with your spouse, what is your goal—to get him/her to do something for you, or to share yourself?

7. Has anyone ever validated your emotions and your experiences? What did it mean to you, and how did it affect your relationship with that person?

CHAPTER 9

— DREAMING —
A Vision for a
Brighter Tomorrow

We are such stuff
As dreams are made on.
—William Shakespeare

"Far away in the sunshine are my highest aspirations," wrote Louisa
May Alcott. "I may not reach them, but I can look up and see their
beauty, believe in them, and try to follow where they lead." What
we imagine about ourselves, our spouse, and our circumstances is
extremely influential in determining where we will end up. Imagination is the creative thrust from within our being that compels us
to reach beyond what we already know exists; it's the stuff dreams
are made of.

Possibilities find their conception in our ideas, and their birth becomes the design of our fantasies. Said John Steinbeck, "Ideas are like rabbits. You get a couple, learn how to handle them, and pretty soon you have a dozen." Those dreams birthed in our imagination can become a wide array of colors used by God to paint our lives and our marriages into something pleasing to him, enjoyable and meaningful to us, and motivating to others.

Engaging in your real love story is a lofty goal and a worthwhile pursuit; it begins with a dream. Hopes and fantasies are windows to our soul, exposing who we are and what we hope to become. Dreams come in many shapes and sizes, but regarding their importance they play a significant role in shaping the course of our life. Proverbs tells us that people perish without vision (29:18 KJV). Dreams are essential to all areas of life: body, soul, spirit . . . and relationships. People can even suffer significant health problems if they don't get enough rapid-eye-movement (REM) sleep, the sleep state where dreaming takes place.

Whether a daydream, a lifelong vision, or a wistful hope, I believe dreams can come true. Someone once watched an eagle effortlessly glide over the treetops and thought, *Wow, if only I could fly like that.* Then, on a warm summer's night, another sat on a porch swing, gazing at the sky and thinking, *I wonder if someday we could put man on the moon?* Still another sat on a park bench in springtime watching a breeze dance around two young lovers walking hand in hand, reminding their observer that one day his dream might become reality. Our hopes and dreams and visions for tomorrow can open our hearts and minds to receive inspiration of what can someday be. Even our earliest dreams of marriage begin with the imagination of splendid possibilities.

The Thrill of Infatuation

As natural as imagination may be, we often fear the magnetic pull of passion and the arousing energy of intrigue. Our whole lives we've heard, "Don't look! Don't touch! Don't imagine!" It may come as a surprise then that, realized in its purest form, infatuation is a very good thing. All wonderful gifts have the potential to bless or to destroy, to be used for good or for evil. What we choose to do with this initial awakening will determine the outcome.

Infatuation is the seed from which all great love stories grow. A closer look at what occurs during infatuation can provide help and hope for creating dreams to sustain romance in marriage. Infatuation consists of two parts; both are important for moving a relationship forward.

The first element of infatuation is fantasy. When we first see someone to whom we're attracted, we begin to anticipate who he or she is and what it might be like to be with him or her. We can get totally caught up in the fantasy, and as time goes on our wishful thinking moves to imagining and dreaming about how our lives might be and feel when we're together. Many times this isn't even a conscious thought, but if a person is asked the right questions he or she can generally identify the early fantasies that have been sculpted.

We have a mindset that the fantasy portion of infatuation is bad, but *fantasy is not always negative.* Obviously, there are numerous situations where indulging in the world of make-believe can be dangerous and destructive. I believe, however, that these initial attractions serve an important role in moving two people toward one another as they consider with bright optimism the possibility of a future together. Hope serves a powerful purpose in both society and relationships. The highest advances in civilization we enjoy today began as a dream in someone's mind.

If, on the other hand, we become too attached to our ideal mental picture of the future, we'll be set up for endless disappointment and frustration. When reality, then, ultimately proves to be different from our fantasy, we tend to think, *Hey, this isn't how it was supposed to be.* Our real-life scenarios aren't matching what we've come to expect and even demand.

Being able to recognize and limit the extent to which we allow fantasy to hold sway can lessen the blow to a relationship that reality often seems to give. My advice is this: Allow the fantasy to motivate, but don't clutch it so tightly that you become imprisoned by it. We must hold our fantasies loosely enough to allow reality to take its rightful place.

The second component of infatuation is the excitement of getting to know someone new and the joy of having him or her be fascinated in return. This too has a tendency to lessen over time as we begin to feel there is less and less to discover about one another. Unlike with fantasy, however, this part of a romantic relationship can last and continue to grow over a lifetime. Whereas our fantasy will be compelled to take a backseat to what we know is real, there's always more we can learn about our spouse, ourselves, and the relationship we share.

A worthwhile exercise for couples can be to review some of their earliest visions for marriage. Since it's so important to keep the dreaming alive and ongoing, a jaunt down memory lane can help refocus ambitions that have gone off course or kick-start an imaginative engine that has stalled. Keep in mind that you may be tempted to blame your spouse for unrealized hopes, and remember: A real love story is one that embraces the full reality of life, including disappointments. The purpose of remembering is to help you stay connected to possibilities for the future and thus help you continue moving forward toward finding Ever After. The pictures you paint in your mind about where you're heading will always look different from the real scenery when you arrive.

Dreaming Together

Sadly, adulthood often drops the curtain on creative imaginations; the hopes and dreams of our youth frequently become distant memories.

"Was my call overseas only a pipe dream?"

"I wanted to design beautiful buildings."

"I thought I could make a difference in the world."

Are these shortsighted examples of youthful idealism? I don't think so.

One reason many couples lose hope of fulfilling a dream is that whenever we talked about reaching for our intended destiny, we pictured arriving there as an individual. Our whole lives we've been told we can be anything we wish to be. As little children we'd read pop-up books and watch TV shows about what we wanted to be when we grew up. When asked, we'd answer, "A policeman, a sailor, a nurse, a fireman, a doctor, an astronaut, a garbage collector," and so forth. As we grew, professionals would come to school and tell us about their jobs. Over and over we were encouraged to set our sights high: "Be anything you want to be!"

But how many of us were ever encouraged to envision being whatever it was we wanted to be *in tandem with our spouse?* We probably imagined being married, but somehow in our fantasy, Husband or Wife was always thrilled to be jogging alongside our destiny or meeting us at the door with dinner ready.

The psychology of winning and inspirational quotes from career gurus encourage and motivate us to reach for the stars, but we must ask ourselves if, just maybe, a part of our destiny is missing. Are we being set up for having our expectations compromised or even lost when one person's dreams meet another's? Not only do we as individuals need to aspire to our full potential, we as couples need to daydream—together.

Brian and Rachel had stars in their eyes when they first married. They both loved the outdoors, and much of their courting was done while hiking, biking, and canoeing. Their dream home would be a log cabin in the wilderness where they'd spend hours talking and planning. The relationship, which began with passion and intensity, is now seriously floundering, and both are secretly considering the end of their five-year marriage.

Rachel thought the birth of their daughter a year ago would be a boost to their relationship, and their sweet Addie did bring their hearts together . . . for a while. But, as before, she and Brian seem to have settled into routines that leave little time for anything close to a meaningful couple connection. While dating they never seemed at a loss for engaging dialogue. Now the only time they speak is when relaying information about the house, their schedules, and their daughter's needs.

To make matters worse, Brian recently purchased a four-wheeler without consulting Rachel. He now spends most of his Saturdays out with his guy friends. When she protests his new favorite pastime, his only response is that he works hard all week and needs a release on the weekends. He says it's the only time he really enjoys himself.

Sam and Robin have had challenges too. They've been married four years; Sam's brothers complain that he isn't available to do as many family things like golfing and fishing anymore. Sam feels torn. He enjoys being with his brothers, but he and Robin clash repeatedly over how to spend their time, how to choose which extended-family activities they'll participate in, and where to draw the line.

Sam and Robin live in the same community where they both grew up. With large families who love to be together, they have more weekly activities than they can possibly attend. They literally could be doing something with family three to four times a week and still not catch all the events. Most recently, Robin's parents started complaining about the couple's plan to have their own private Thanksgiving dinner before coming to the parents' house later in the day.

This young couple felt torn about a number of such issues, and more kept surfacing. Feeling pulled in different directions, Sam and Robin had exchanged harsh words, which left them both feeling hurt and increasingly hopeless about dealing peacefully with family matters. Finally, while attempting to work through this conflict, Robin recalled a conversation they'd had during their engagement when they agreed to make sure their marriage had priority over other family relationships. They'd known then that both families would compete for their time and attention. As they talked, they came to realize how impossible it was to keep everybody happy. They decided that in order to prioritize their marriage, sometimes they might have to disappoint their families and even risk misunderstanding.

Consequently, Sam and Robin began to feel a renewed sense of commitment to their relationship. They're proud of themselves for taking the time to sort it out and work it through. Of course, they both love their families, and while they recognize family members won't always appreciate or understand their decisions, they resolved to keep time for themselves. Even though they still feel some stress and tension, the experience of renewing their commitment to their agreed-upon values and priorities gave them a stronger sense of purpose and commitment to making their marriage great.

See the contrast between these two couples? Both struggling, but Sam and Robin seemed to have turned a corner, while Brian and Rachel seem headed in opposite ways. One key difference is how the couples set up expectations for their futures. Dreaming is an important part of dating, and it's useful throughout a marriage. However, we're not only talking here about wistful, fantasy-like dreaming. As previously stated, while that type of imagination for the two of you can be enjoyable and motivating, valuable dreams can come in various other forms. Let's take a closer look.

Not only have Brian and Rachel squared off as adversaries, but they're also sorely lacking a clear sense of vision for their marriage.

They lack a set of mutually agreed-upon priorities to return to and reaffirm when they run into challenges. They entered their marriage with great hopes for the future together and a general desire to be "happy." Beyond that they figured they'd deal with the details when they arrived.

How many couples struggle because they've abandoned the values and priorities they established early on? How many couples actually never take the opportunity to share and solidify mutual dreams, core values, and priorities? At NIM we find that couples who cultivate together a sense of purpose and mission in life possess advantages over couples who allow circumstances to determine their priorities for them.

It's not that people enter marriage without values and dreams. Instead it's the deep heartfelt, *unspoken* passions of two individuals that set them up for conflict, distrust, and discouragement. Or, if the couple did spend time brainstorming together, they may not have taken the time to mutually affirm a common set of clearly agreed-upon goals for their marriage. Perhaps they have no idea what to do when the inevitable conflicts unexpectedly emerge. All three situations are extremely common; the good news is that with a bit of cooperation each scenario is easy to change.

Couples who dream together are more likely to keep their values and aspirations in the forefront of their planning and decision-making. The ability to look forward and pursue those aspirations is what separates relationships that are *going* places from relationships that are *being taken* hostage by their circumstances. For some, hopes come crashing down immediately, such as when the loaded-with-specific-expectations wedding and honeymoon prove to be enormous setups for disappointment.

Your dreams may have chipped away so gradually that you now spend what little time you do think about your marriage figuring out how to readjust your expectations down to almost nothing.

Wherever you find yourself on the continuum, it's not hard to identify with the deflated emotions that come with the loss of a vision. In fact, most people don't realize this is one of the most powerful forms of grief.

Grieving is all about loss, but because we're talking about the imagined, we often don't feel we can justify the feelings. We tell ourselves our emotions are stupid; after all, we're mourning something that wasn't even real. In contrast, again, dreams play a substantial role in our lives and have much to do with building momentum and motivating us forward. They help us find our meaning and purpose, and they often give us the incentive we need to strive through the challenges toward a goal worthy of our life's investment.

The loss of a dream is a real and legitimate loss, and the resulting grief is real grief. Your hopes for your marriage were, and are, important. Discovering and committing to your ideals for a glorious tomorrow can reinvigorate a lifeless relationship and give much-needed direction to what presently may seem to be an aimless quest.

Embracing Change

Change takes but an instant. It's the resistance
to change that can take a lifetime.
—Hebrew Proverb

Another important element in understanding the journey of dreams is that our aspirations normally change and evolve over time. How can couples possibly stay current with each other if they're not dreaming together? Many marriages crumble under the realization that husband and wife have drifted so far apart over time they have little in common. They felt connected to their victories in the beginning but apparently have traveled down different paths and

(1) didn't see it coming, (2) didn't know it would become a problem, or (3) didn't know what to do about it. A huge part of staying close and connected is disclosing and exploring each other's expectations *across a lifetime*. Being alive, by definition, involves constant change. Moving waters are not stagnant. If both partners aren't growing and changing, something is dead or dying. You typically don't need to fear the loss of your spouse to his or her aspirations if you move together.

A key, then, to staying motivated on the sojourn together is remaining engaged in the process of assisting each other in realizing your tomorrows—both as individuals and as a couple. I pointed out earlier that in marriage there are three concurrent journeys—yours, your spouse's, and your marriage's—and that all three deserve careful attention. Each provides an opportunity to be part of the adventurous romance. Remember (from chapter 2) the husband who said, "If I pursued my dreams, the kids and the house would have to go"? Making room in your life and relationship for your passions or fancies to be valued and pursued can keep beliefs like these from taking root and becoming the prevailing mood of your marriage.

I realize that I could be accused of writing about sharing our hopes and dreams with our spouses as if it were a simple, risk-free proposition. I know that's not the case! Looking to tomorrow holds some of our most private and vulnerable yearnings. Dreams are often spun with fantasies about possibilities that don't currently exist, at least not for you. They may even represent situations that others think are silly or impossible because they involve creative thought and forward thinking. Or someone might think you're presumptuous to believe you could have such a thing or pull off such an outlandish feat. We're often met with full-frontal opposition: "If it hasn't been done before, what makes you think it can be done?"

I have a close friend and colleague who has his PhD in psychology. His professional aspirations went way beyond anything members of his rural family had previously done. He was criticized all along the way for being full of himself, for believing he could accomplish his goal. We come to a crossroads wherein we ask ourselves, *Do I dare disclose my wishes if they will be criticized, judged, or ridiculed?*

Dream conversations should be treated with the utmost care and sensitivity. Notice how important safety in the relationship is to this process. Like other dimensions discussed in this book, the care and safety with which dreams are attended is pivotal in living a romantic adventure.

One way we might hinder the important role of dreaming in our marriage journey relates to the posture we take toward our own dreams. For instance, we may hold our vision (or calling) so tightly we won't let go. It's possible to be so rigidly committed and confined to our dream that we make it a higher priority than the relationship itself. I'm sure you know of people who believe the well-being of spouse and family are up for compromise as long as he or she doesn't sacrifice the pursuit of success. And the other extreme is no better: If we don't value our dreams at all, they may be nothing more than passing thoughts and fail to appreciably impact the direction of our lives.

Several years ago a couple in distress entered therapy looking for guidance on how to get their new marriage on track. The husband, I'll call him Bill, was in his late thirties and this was his first marriage. The wife, I'll call her Cindy, was also in her late thirties but had been married and divorced and had a teenage daughter. Bill and Cindy had been married less than a year and were having significant conflict. Both reported that their courtship and engagement had been enjoyable and satisfying, and they were disappointed to discover that their once harmonious relationship became contentious after stepping away from the altar.

Bill explained that during their yearlong engagement they had meticulously planned for what life would be like once they married.

They had long discussions about finances, division of household chores, parenting, and more. There was scarcely an issue they hadn't reviewed and discussed while preparing. While Bill was telling his side of the story, frustration kept building in his voice and soon his face went scarlet. He concluded by exclaiming, "And she hasn't kept any of our agreements!"

When Cindy was asked if this was how she saw it, she looked puzzled and, with a shrug, said, "I changed my mind."

She couldn't understand his fury. For her, their discussions about the future all made sense at the time, but expectations were conditional for her. She was so flexible that any presenting circumstance challenging their previously set plans was reason to toss off the agreement in favor of addressing new factors as they surfaced.

On the other hand, Bill was so rigidly committed to his ideals it never occurred to him that flexibility would be an asset to the marriage. For him any deviation from their chartered course represented a failure of character and left him feeling insecure about the relationship.

Bill and Cindy illustrate the need for flexibility, whether designing lifelong ambitions or merely laying out daily tasks. Our dreams are critical to setting course for the romantic adventure, and that course will surely be tested by circumstance. For some values we must fight to the bitter end. But others will evolve and be shaped by changing circumstances. Without an ongoing dialogue designating which ones are which, couples wind up being carried along by situations and are vulnerable to feelings of resentment, betrayal, and despair.

Focusing Your Dreams

A number of dream types can end up being useful to you in guiding and invigorating your life and marriage. Daydreams can be fanciful trips into our imagination, whether tied to reality or filled with the elements of fairy tales. Dreams that occur during sleep can take many forms, from the surreal to the supernatural and almost anything else imaginable. They're often surprising and can open our minds to things we've never before considered.

Envisioning the future can also take the form of creative planning and exploring personal desires and possibilities. All these forms of reverie can be useful sources of information, possibility, and motivation, but what we specifically want to discuss here is how to focus your dreams in order to be able to take full advantage of the opportunities they provide for achieving an inspired marriage.

Toward that ultimate end, it's important to clarify the function imagination plays. You see, dreams themselves have the potential to be interesting and exciting on their own. The type of dreaming we want to address is for the purpose of not only keeping the marriage exciting but also of providing an inspired direction to help guide you both forward—a looking to the future that brings focus to your marital journey and assists in connecting to a goal you both can enthusiastically embrace.

If you're ready to engage the idea of intentionally seeking a meaningful direction for your marriage, it's generally useful to begin with some questions. It isn't necessary to answer any or all of these formally. Their purpose is to help you think intentionally about your marriage and where it's heading. You will likely come up with plenty of your own questions once you get started. As an exercise for you and your spouse, you may want to answer some of these individually, then share and compare answers together.

Starting with the basics, you may ask yourself:

- What is marriage?
- Why get married?
- What is the purpose or point of marriage?
- What hopes, aspirations, and purposes will be fulfilled while living as a married person that I wouldn't somehow have as a single person?

- What do I personally feel makes a marriage ideal?
- What do I think is my spouse's view of an ideal marriage?
- What is God's perspective on marriage?
- Why did God create the institution of marriage, and toward what end?
- What is God's dream for our marriage?
- In what ways does a successful Christ-centered marriage impact God's kingdom?
- What role does marriage play in raising healthy, well-adjusted children?
- Do successful marriages impact the community, the nation, the world, in meaningful ways? If so, how?

Again, I love great questions, but rather than continue formulating them here, I want to present this as a possible starting point. I hope you'll seize the opportunity to allow your mind and spirit to stretch while you seriously think through these ideas. I've been doing so for years and have yet to exhaust the possibilities.

Your ability to come up with your own personal blueprint for your life and marriage may be greater than you realize. You may need to allow yourself to start simply. If you're learning to play the piano, it's fine to start with *Mary Had a Little Lamb*. As a couple you might begin with a rousing duet of *Chopsticks*. Most inspiring accomplishments have humble beginnings. Give each other grace. A consistent investment of time, energy, and prayer can be leveraged into something magnificent with a little divine assistance.

I will leave you to your choices about what you want to do with these suggestions. Many times I've asked myself and others similar questions and have found startling truth I'd never before considered. When I ask, "Why get married?" or "What's the point of marriage?" a common answer from men is, "Sex." I've had many men tell me that sex is the only thing they can't righteously have outside of marriage.

I wholeheartedly reject that idea! Here's the reason: That answer is all about "getting," and I don't believe the primary reason I was created was "to get." Don't hear me wrong, I love "getting." I just know there has to be more to my purpose for marriage than that. As I've already indicated, in the early years of my marriage I didn't really know why I got married other than that I wanted a family and someone to share my life . . . and yes, I wanted sex. I'm not meaning to suggest that those are bad reasons to get hitched, but I've since come to see my life and marriage more in terms of allowing all I was created to be to find full expression in this world. And not just to shine personally; the image of Christ in me was yearning for opportunity to be expressed.

Allowing Christ's light to shine through me means I get to see and experience him making a difference. And I believe more light is better when we're talking about the light of Christ. One of my personal aspirations, then, is to find as many ways as I can to be a shining light in a world filled with darkness and despair. I know this is oversimplified, but my life makes more sense when I see it this way.

I've also come to believe that I am fundamentally a relational being, patterned after my Lord, who is relational to his core. My life is made full as I live it out in companionship with others. In fact, associating with others seems to increase the potential for my light to shine even brighter, and my marriage is the best place for this. When Jenni and I are doing well as a couple, my soul's generator revs up and my beacon of light shines brighter and extends further.

Jenni is not only my motivator but also my journeying partner in loving and learning. We learn together about life, love, God, ourselves, each other, and how we can make a meaningful difference. I could go it alone, but I have no desire to do so. I love helping her discover and realize her personal dreams too. I thrive on the romance and adventure of living life with her. I don't always know what God is doing in the big picture with my life and marriage, but I do have a strong sense that it truly matters.

A Marriage Mission Statement

Another exercise you may find useful in helping focus your marriage dreams is to crystallize your overarching direction and purpose into a single declaration. What we're talking about is the equivalent of a marriage mission statement. Many corporations and organizations spend enormous amounts of energy formulating their purpose. Most business experts believe a clear, compelling articulation of a mission statement may be an enterprise's greatest asset for success.

Jack Herschend is Chairman of the Board for the NIM. His company, Herschend Family Entertainment, owns or manages some of the nation's most successful theme parks, including Silver Dollar City in Missouri, Dollywood in Tennessee, and Stone Mountain in Georgia. One of the characteristic raves about their parks is not only how fun and family oriented the experience is, but also how happy, caring, and respectful the employees are. The company's statement of purpose reflects a top-down commitment that permeates their parks from the inside out: "We create memories worth repeating." Beyond that is an articulation of core values that together with the mission statement guides and influences how they do business and conduct relationships within and without.

If mission statements have this much power in the corporate world, is it possible there's something here to help couples shape their journey toward vitality and success? Corporations consist of relationships that must function smoothly and efficiently. I believe the importance of a declaration of direction and purpose is just as powerful for a man and a woman. Would you approach your marriage any differently if your own mission statement was "to create memories worth repeating"?

Here are several sample "marriage mission statements" to spur your thinking:

(1) Our marriage affords us the opportunity to become all that God created us to be.

(2) We are committed to spending our lives in service to others together for the glory of God.

(3) This family will be a refuge from all that's wrong and bad in the world and a celebration of all that's right and good within us.

(4) To create a Christ-centered marriage we both enjoy, where we share Christ's love and glorify him.

(5) Together our lives are worship to God through our dedication to working hard, playing well, resting thoroughly, and thus offering love and peace to each other and our world.

Notice how each statement might provide course correction and perspective when life circumstances become challenging. A couple who settled on the first marriage mission statement might think doubly hard about the husband accepting a promotion that might mean more money but would take him out of activities that make use of his talents in working with people and serving their needs. A couple with the third mission statement might be inspired to join a mission effort to reclaim a portion of the inner city, becoming a beacon for Christ in a troubled part of their community. Do you see how much impact a marriage mission statement could have?

To formulate yours, consider the following steps:

(1) Search your own heart for where your passions lie. What do you privately dream about? What are your heart's desires, those perhaps placed within you by God himself?

(2) Can you care about what your spouse's secret hopes might be? Are you prepared to listen and care about his/her dreams even if at first they appear to be a threat to your own?

(3) Seek an opportunity for Heart Talk about each other's aspirations.

(4) Identify the areas of common passion and vision in your dreams.

(5) Attempt separately to summarize your dreams and values in a single sentence.

(6) Compare your efforts and see if you can combine them into a meaningful statement.

(7) Consider displaying this statement where you will see it often and may even be asked by others to explain its meaning. (This is a great way to hold each other accountable to your marriage mission.)

(8) Set a date to reexamine your mission statement to see if it needs alteration or updating.

Don't be too concerned about the statement's eloquence. This is *your* marriage mission statement. Ultimately, it only needs to make sense to you, your spouse, and God. The power in this discipline is in helping you to remain focused and fresh about the purpose of your romantic adventure. Invite God into the process. Allow your heavenly Father, who loves you deeply, to celebrate with you in the fulfillment of the dreams he has placed within you.

Conclusion

My life's journey with Jenni began with infatuation. I imagined our flawless future together, and for years I fought letting go of fantasy when reality's disappointments attempted to mess up my dream. When I finally began to allow real life to take its rightful place and my picture of our future to be altered by the truth, life became remarkably easier. Your own romance can take a turn for the better when you can allow both your dreams and discoveries to motivate and compel you onward. Hold your dreams lightly enough to let go when reality shows up. You are then freed to embark again on the path to exploration and fascination. Reclaim your Ever After—it's yours for the taking.

Antoine de Saint-Exupéry, twentieth-century French aviator, writer, and real-life hero, penned these words: "If you want to build a ship, don't drum up people to collect wood and don't assign them tasks and work, but rather *teach them to long for the endless immensity of the sea.*"[1] When forming and thinking about our aspirations—the vision of a bright tomorrow—we can easily become focused on the wood, on the nuts and bolts of making it all happen, and the task can begin to feel altogether too much like work. With all we've discussed here, my greatest hope is that we don't forget that for which we yearn: "the endless immensity of the sea."

————— *to* **Ponder** *and* **Discuss** —————

1. When you dream about the future, are you more like Bill or more like Cindy?

2. What have you previously believed was the purpose or point of marriage for you, and how is that belief developing or changing?

3. Do you see marriage and family as more of an asset in the ability to realize your dreams, or more of a hindrance?

4. When dealing with dreams, what would you hope to get out of marriage that you would not get from being single?

5. What do you personally feel makes a marriage ideal? What do you think is your spouse's view of an ideal marriage?

6. What do you believe is God's perspective on marriage? In what ways does a successful, Christ-centered marriage impact the kingdom of God?

7. What elements would you be excited to have in your personal marriage mission statement?

CHAPTER 10

—PURSUING—
Making Your Dreams
a Reality

*If you have built castles in the air, your work need
not be lost; that is where they should be.
Now put foundations under them.*
—Henry David Thoreau

Dreams in themselves can be exciting and energizing; sharing those
dreams can connect a couple in meaningful and intimate ways. The
experience of being on the same team, committed to shared goals,
can be a continual source of life and vitality. However, while many
people are adept at dreaming, far fewer know how to take dreams
beyond imagination into reality. For dreams to continue to energize
and propel couples from mediocrity to greatness, team effort
toward making the dream come true must accompany the vision.

One of the greatest sources of energy comes through the pursuit itself.

Many couples find that working together poses unique, hard-to-manage challenges; Jenni and I (both stubborn and strong-willed) are no exception. In spite of ourselves, though, we've excelled in one area that can spell virtual relationship death: home improvement.

Years ago we bought a house that had been a rental for seventeen years; it was structurally sound but badly in need of updating. We both had a vision of making our home a beautiful sanctuary and were anxious to dive in. Because our budget was tight, do-it-yourself was the only option.

At one point we decided to replace the horribly ugly brown and orange linoleum with bright ceramic tile. Neither of us had ever laid tile before, but the book made it look so easy.

We could only work on it in our spare time, so we knew we'd be inconvenienced for a week or so. Our kitchen would be unusable—the cooking range would be parked in the garage, the refrigerator and dining room table moved into the living room. Oh, by the way, did I mention we had four children between the ages of one and eleven . . . and we were home-schooling? This project was in the early chapter—the one before we'd had enough experience to realize home-improvement jobs generally take two to three times longer than expected—so our one-week timeline proved slightly optimistic.

Well, we dove in. We planned it all out, prepared the floor, and laid the cement board foundation. Following the advice of a well-meaning neighbor, a self-proclaimed do-it-yourself expert, we used screws instead of nails (for added quality), which would add a little time to the project. We mapped out our grid of four-inch squares and proceeded to use my handy portable drill for all two thousand screws. Time was of the essence until, unexpectedly, the bargain drill didn't have enough torque to countersink the screw heads, which would mean disaster when we laid the tile.

I got the first four hundred screws to within a quarter inch of home; then, at midnight, Jenni and I attempted to do the rest by hand. Two A.M. came and went; my arm was cramping so badly I was ready to give up. I was exhausted and my mood was foul, but Jenni continued pressing on. Just as the sun was coming up, we turned in for a couple hours of sleep before the kids woke.

To finish, we had to rent a high-powered drill. After readjusting our timeline for completion and our lifestyle for inconvenience, *one long month later* the floor was done, and, I must say, it looked beautiful. We felt an overwhelming sense of accomplishment with having made our dream a reality.

By the way, the very next month, our neighbor—the one who recommended the screws—had a professional come and install *their* new tile floor. In three days.

Jenni and I have now worked years at becoming an efficient team and through much pain and toil have successfully undertaken and accomplished many types of projects. In this chapter of life I could be tempted to coast into "relational retirement" and enjoy the fruits of our labor, but I know too much about what it took to get here and what it takes to stay here. I want to remain engaged in the adventure and the romance, staying inspired and alive.

Taking it easy may have its benefits, and I'm not condemning those who have retired, but many people view ending employment as the beginning of a long-awaited life of leisure. Often the unconscious desire is to escape a relatively meaningless workaday existence to enter an equally meaningless but hopefully more enjoyable time of relaxation, play, and travel.

Disappointment is common, and for many folks retirement turns out to be merely biding time until they pass on. The reality is, many work their entire life dreaming of a joyous retirement only to die within the first year. Draw your own conclusions about why this so commonly occurs, but I'm convinced that we were meant to stay meaningfully engaged and invested in life's adventure and romance, continuing to invest in the unfolding of God's kingdom. Therefore, I never want to coast through a relational retirement. I plan to keep working on and investing in my marriage. As long as the opportunity exists, I will continue pursuing the dream of finding Ever After.

Relational Consumer, or Relational Investor?

Continuing to invest in your relationship is central to having and maintaining a great marriage. There's no other way I know to make your dreams become a reality. Unfortunately, one of the great unseen threats to the goal of creating an awesome marriage is the result of an underlying value of our culture that has wormed its way into our relationships. We've become a consumer-oriented society with nearly unparalleled affluence. We're accustomed to conveniences and comforts once thought of as luxuries but now considered reasonable expectations. Increasingly, we want it now—we'll pay for it later.

Whether luxuries *or* reasonable expectations, we're used to having most of our needs and many of our wants satisfied. As a result we're not only inclined but encouraged toward discontentment; we want more! I likewise am a product of this society so I'm not judging it; I merely want to point out how our mindset is impacting our marriages.

Hollywood regularly produces movies that reflect the culture's prevailing attitude and beliefs. On a good day, they also challenge us to reflect on and perhaps rethink some of the values we've adopted. In *Bruce Almighty,* Jim Carrey is a self-absorbed, irreverent TV news reporter from Buffalo. The egocentric Bruce is obsessed with his career and hyper-focused on why he keeps getting passed over for promotion. Feeling utterly victimized, his underlying complaint is "Why do others get what they want but not me?" When he again doesn't get the anchor job he wants, he snaps and descends into a violent bout of self-pity. Livid with God, he screams, "Why do you hate me?"

His vision of the Almighty is deeply skewed. He describes God as "a mean kid sitting on an anthill with a magnifying glass." Bruce shakes his fist toward heaven, criticizing God's administration and pronouncing God unjust for failing to bring about the fulfillment of his desires. Then God meets Bruce and gives him a chance to demonstrate how much better "Bruce Almighty" can run the world than God Almighty. Bruce has to learn, the hard and humorous way, that there's far more to life than just getting what he thinks he wants.

Whatever we do or don't have in common with Bruce, with shocking precision he exemplifies the materialistic mindset we all know too well. The consumer's goal is to consume—to get as much as possible, savor it, and then get some more. One may work hard for what's obtained, but getting is the goal.

The next logical step in a commodity-oriented society is to become an "accomplished" consumer. If we're going to do something, why not do it well? Therefore, in the name of efficiency, we also prize getting more with less effort. An extreme example of this is found in one of today's most popular fantasies: winning the lottery. How many people have elaborate dreams of the jackpot? Have you ever sat and tried to imagine what you'd do if you suddenly had all that money? Again, my aim is not to judge right or wrong, but instead to highlight how this cultural emphasis can play out in marriage.

Our consumer orientation influences us to approach our marriages the same way. When answering the dream questions in chapter 9, how many of your initial thoughts about "why get married?"

had something to do with what you wanted or hoped to get out of the deal? Most people I know consciously or unconsciously view marriage as a place to get their needs met. And many of us unconsciously hope we won't have to do *too* much to get it—the cost shouldn't be higher than the reward. Since this is what we're taught to expect, why would we think otherwise?

We're generally willing to meet the needs of our spouse so the pursuit doesn't seem overly selfish or self-centered. But upon looking a little closer you might notice the underlying consumerist mantra: The goal is "to get." Thus, if your spouse isn't meeting your needs, you might label the relationship as "not working out." If you primarily gauge the success of your marriage by what you and your spouse are getting out of it, you have a consumer orientation.

The alternative is to approach your marriage as an investor. In contrast to that of a consumer, the investor's expectation is to build and grow assets. Receiving benefits after making a contribution is fine, but the underlying goal of growing something changes the attitude toward the endeavor and changes how success is measured. How would marriage look from an investment viewpoint?

Have you ever put time and money into a fixer-upper house or a small business? If so, you can relate to our story above and have most likely experienced firsthand the ups and downs of an investment growing over time. What many of us don't understand is that our marriages require this same kind of sacrifice if we hope to see our dreams come true. With a house or business venture, returns on the investment are fairly tangible. We see a profit when that first fixer-upper house is sold or we can track the venture's financial performance. Profit-and-return on a marriage is far more subjective. Those of us investing in a Christ-centered marriage will want to judge success by criteria beyond profits or gains.

Serious investors select an enterprise worthy of their investment and commit on the basis of a principle or purpose larger than even the enterprise itself. It's not that they don't note the lack of return; rather, short-term gain or profit is only one of many factors determining the success of their investment. The investment isn't predicated on simple gratification.

In this book we've been talking about pursuing the dream of constructing a marriage that you both can enjoy and that makes a difference in the world *simply by being a great marriage*. The investment made includes: time, attention, energy, love, and care. The commitment is to both the marriage and to the people involved.

It's wonderful when one's contributions are paying big dividends, but this is merely a nice byproduct. Success should be defined by whether a loving relationship is developing and whether the couple's goals and mission are being accomplished. A strong sense of core values underlies all they do, and hopefully their definition of success will also include appreciation of their marriage's contribution to building God's kingdom.

Examples of value-centered investing are sources of motivation and inspiration to me. Seeing what makes them work, thrive, and contribute to the kingdom is interesting in a broad business sense, but they also help me see possibilities for my marriage. One of my favorites is the Chick-fil-A Corporation. I love their chicken sandwich, but another reason I like them is that I've had the privilege of working directly with them and their nonprofit foundation, Winshape (named for the underlying goal of shaping winners).

I've gotten to know the people who run the company and have been amazed at their deep commitment to an unusual value system. More than being motivated by profit margins, leaders are committed to investing in people and their families as well as the cause of Christ. In fact, their corporate mission is "To glorify God by being a faithful steward of all that is entrusted to us and to have a positive influence on all that come in contact with Chick-fil-A."

They're pursuing an exciting and noble dream. And, with a people-centered rather than profit-centered focus, they've built a two-billion-dollar company without having to sacrifice or compromise their core values. Their concern for running a successful business is always secondary to investing in people and the kingdom. One of the more well-known examples is Chick-fil-A's long-standing commitment to remaining closed on Sundays. Through this policy they sacrifice millions of dollars annually; however, their attitude is not that money is being lost but rather that capital is being endowed in the families of those who work with the company.

A look inside the company reveals how their value of investing in people permeates everything they do and extends far beyond the Chick-fil-A family. For instance, founder Truitt Cathy has built, managed, and funded a foster-care program that's provided safe, secure, and loving homes for hundreds of children who would otherwise be largely forgotten. These are just two samples; the scope of Chick-fil-A's commitment to making an eternal investment is far too extensive to cover here. The point is, they're focused on investment in what the Lord loves and making a meaningful contribution to things of eternal value.

My marriage has eternal value and is worth this same level of devotion. Likewise, for it to grow into something awesome, it needs to be consistently invested in and nurtured. If I'm a gardener and my goal is to create a beautiful garden, I may work years to make it just right. I'll plan the landscape, plant trees and shrubs and flowers, and carefully tend to it all. And I'll make sure there are truckloads of fertilizer!

With careful attention, my garden will become a sight to behold and a pleasure to experience. I guarantee I will get great joy and satisfaction from what's been accomplished. Sharing it with others will be satisfying to me and hopefully to them. If, however, I then begin to leave my now-perfect garden unattended, to fend for itself, it will become overgrown, and shortly there will be little evidence that a garden ever existed.

One day a preacher happened upon a man tending a beautiful garden. The preacher exclaimed, "Look at the marvelous work God and you have done together!"

The gardener replied, "Yes, Reverend, but you should have seen it when God had it to himself."

Don't groan! Marriages function just like gardens. God provides all the raw ingredients needed to make a marriage spectacular and, like the garden, he designed us to manage it (see Genesis 1:26–31). But cultivating the marriage journey into something beautiful, fruitful, and satisfying requires a continual investment of our time and energy. Great gardens don't happen by accident; neither do great marriages. When we work together with God, our marriage can become our own private paradise.

Someone might ask, "But what if I never see any return from my investment in the relationship? How long do I have to wait?" Most married individuals have asked such questions at some point; sadly, though, for some it's a persistent refrain that expresses their deep and abiding disappointment. While there are no definitive answers to these inquiries, there may be a way to address them that sustains hope in the face of prolonged silence.

First, *wanting returns on your investment is not a bad thing.* "Why am I not seeing more results from my efforts in this marriage?" is a valid question. So, letting go of the question is not necessarily the place to begin. Asking expresses a belief that the relationship could be something more than what it currently is; and, again, God wants this also.

It's completely reasonable to want your marriage to provide love, affection, friendship, and passion. Just like it's appropriate to want your life in general to be full, satisfying, and meaningful. Most of us enter marriage hoping for those things. When the dreams go unfulfilled we experience *genuine* grief and disappointment, and the process of learning how to manage these feelings deserves the tender hand of God's love and mercy as well as your own.

Your deep emotional needs deserve attention. But the pertinent question here is whether you're approaching your marriage as an investor or a consumer. "Am I in this to get what I want now, or am I attempting to put in for the long haul, toward some greater value or purpose?"

Second, you may want to examine your expectations by asking, *"What sort of returns am I really looking for?"* Sometimes evidence of a new beginning or a slight return on relationship investment has been overlooked because we want dramatic results. I can miss indications of change in my relationship because of how narrowly I've defined the desired gains or how desperately I've wanted something specific. Not only could evidence of the return be missed, but my limited definition might be excluding returns of great value to me.

Consider the value of personal integrity and character. Is growth in my own integrity and character a worthwhile return for investing in a relationship? In my marriage, I've learned countless lessons in how to be a man of love and integrity through both the good times and the hard times. Many of the most powerful lessons have developed through adversity. I don't normally enjoy the process of getting there, but I appreciate the results of becoming a better man, a man I feel great about being.

What's the primary return on investment most spouses expect? *Change.* They contribute to the relationship over and over hoping for some sort of change . . . *in their partner.* If there's no evidence, they despair and conclude that their sacrifice was for nothing, so they stop.

Consider the scenario of a wife who's been repeatedly hurt by her husband's lying. Her expectation for a husband of honesty and integrity is valid, and the resulting security she'd feel is the return she's hoping for. After years of investing in the relationship, she concludes that he'll never change, so she stops investing.

Her bitterness and resentment deepen, and she reasons that since he's not trustworthy, it doesn't matter if she is. Consequently, she withholds information from him and pursues private agendas without his input or knowledge. Maybe she even invests time and emotion into other relationships to the exclusion of the marriage. Can you see where this could go?

Eventually she becomes a different person, one whom, upon reflection, she doesn't like and doesn't want to be. As a result of withholding her investment in the relationship, her own integrity has been jeopardized. In essence she betrays herself and drifts until finally she's as morally compromised as her husband. I wish I could say this is an unusual scenario. Regrettably, these dynamics are played out every day in many marriages.

Let's redefine the type of investment I'm referring to. It can be identified in two parts:

(1) Engaging the pursuit of personal growth toward becoming more and more the person God created you to be.

(2) Devoting your time, energy, interest, emotions, effort (etc.) into your marriage toward a goal or series of objectives that seem significant. This can involve investing in your spouse by assisting him/her in becoming a more complete expression of who he/she was created to be, and/or more fully realize his/her potential.

As inspiring as dreams can be, with minimal or no effort made toward realizing future hopes, dreams quickly lose their power. If one spouse is committed to rolling up his or her sleeves and digging in to the work of making the dreams a reality but the other is not, the act of dreaming together again won't energize the marriage. At that point dreaming is in danger of being resented as escapism, no longer part of a genuine romance or adventure. So what then can we do to make our dreams come true?

Tips for Making Your Dreams Come True

There are some people who live in a dream world, and there are some who face reality; and then there are those who turn one into the other.
—Douglas Everett

As a couple you have an amazing opportunity to take the exciting pictures of possibilities you've painted in your minds and turn them into a reality you've longed to live. In essence, you want to put legs on your dreams so your hopes can become animated—moving, breathing, brought to life. Bringing dreams to reality looks a lot like investing, and investing looks like love.

It would be tempting at this point to suggest a series of simple steps assuring success in the pursuit of your dreams. However, the paths couples travel together on their unique adventures widely vary. Rather than looking for a one-size-fits-all approach, I'd prefer to offer some suggestions you may find useful. This better accounts for rich differences in personality, temperament, preferences, lifestyle, and circumstances that bear on your journey, and it encourages you to customize as necessary.

(1) For the Moment, Focus on One Aspect of Your Vision

It's possible for you to have multiple objectives for your life and marriage, but it helps to think through one at a time. Jenni and I may dream of a marriage that feels safe; we may also be interested in spending our vacation time this year in a way that thrills us both equally; on top of that we might have a vision of being an ongoing source of encouragement and support for our married children as they develop their own families. While it's wonderful for us to have a number of dreams at any one time, trying to address them simultaneously is frustrating and unproductive. Just like two people trying to speak at once doubles the volume yet hinders the communication, trying to clarify multiple dreams at the same time only creates noise and confusion.

(2) Begin With the End in Mind

Steven Covey, who's helped many people become highly effective in varied pursuits, has an important suggestion for any type of goal-setting endeavor: Regarding what you're shooting for, get clear about what and where the target is.[1] Jenni and I may know we want to feel safer together without concern of being embarrassed, judged, or belittled. But how will we know when we've succeeded? Even a small step in the right direction would qualify as being more secure than before, yet this probably wouldn't feel like a dream come true. So we've established that our desire is to feel supremely loved when together—"the safest place in the entire world." We now have a marker to help us gauge our progress.

(3) Develop a Plan

Actually, I've accomplished many things in life lacking a well-thought-out plan; I'm not suggesting this as a requirement. I've even been able to figure out ways to increase Jenni's feeling of safety through observation and trial and error. However, those methods can be slow and inefficient. They can set me up to become discouraged if or when I continually miss the mark, and then I wonder if I'm even making any progress at all.

On the evening I came home determined to be "Joe Romance" I was definitely shooting in the dark. Beginning to find out what made Jenni feel loved or unloved was the beginning of a map to success. I was able to formulate an effective plan to get love from my heart to hers in ways I knew she would welcome. Likewise with our security, if I take the time to begin understanding what we need, I can create a plan for getting there that increases our likelihood of success.

(4) Agree to Be Accountable to Each Other

Dreams have a way of getting lost in the shuffle of daily life. It may not be that we've abandoned the quest—perhaps we've just forgotten or momentarily lost sight of the vision. Maybe a situation presents itself that one of us didn't even realize applied to the dream. For instance, Jenni has told me that when I get upset and raise my voice she doesn't want to share her feelings or hear mine. Sometimes I'm not even aware I've raised my voice, but since I've given her permission to hold me accountable, she can inform me that my tone or volume is not feeling safe. Her reminder doesn't annoy me and make my irritation spiral; I've chosen to let her become a mirror to help me see what would otherwise be hard to recognize and, thus, would hinder our success.

(5) Remain Flexible

Though we're all aware of our circumstances changing over time, we have to make a conscious decision to remain flexible. Sometimes we must adjust to unforeseen events that unexpectedly alter the course of life, such as illness or job loss. Other changes are the result of our previous choices, such as moving. Still others are normal stage-of-life transitions, such as becoming parents. Regardless of what prompts the changes, our dreams will likely be impacted. If we aren't able to adjust our dreams and our approach to fulfilling them, we'll find ourselves at odds with the unfolding adventure and will quickly become frustrated or discouraged. Radical shifts can be exhilarating, but only if we bend and move with them.

Recently as Jen and I have been moving toward the empty-nest phase, our life has encountered a remarkable remodel: Two of our kids are married, one is in college, and our youngest is still at home. After seventeen years of devoting herself to teaching our kids, Jenni is no longer home-schooling and has gone into business for herself. Now working full-time, she one day proudly celebrated her semi-retirement from "domestic engineering." Nate and I looked at each other as the realization of what that really meant for us boys began to sink in. Like it or not, we had to step up to the plate in some new ways.

To honor Jenni and help her feel cared for and appreciated, we've readjusted our domestic responsibilities. We're working even more as a housekeeping team so that nobody (especially Jenni) feels unfairly burdened. She and I still have the same dreams for a great marriage—they haven't changed—but our picture of what this looks like sure has, and our strategies to get there are undergoing a major overhaul.

(6) Allow for Trial and Error

Remember, so much of our growth and our development of useful life skills occurs through trial and error. Learning to successfully pursue our dreams is no exception. A great marriage works for both partners as individuals, and feels good together. Sometimes we know exactly what we want or need, but often we discover it as we go. Many of us have a tendency to hold too tightly to what we believe is necessary for our happiness. We may not even realize we could find unexpected fulfillment through unforeseen alternatives ... until it happens! Adventurous romance at its best leaves plenty of room for surprise.

(7) Accept Disappointment As Part of the Package

Realistically, with all we can do to make our dreams come true, we'll always encounter a measure of disappointment. We were originally designed to live in Eden, and this is not it! Yet something inside all of us still longs for the perfect garden and yearns for our eternal Ever After.

I will do everything I can to make my marriage as close to heaven as possible. For my wife and I to feel safe therein, the truth of our fallen world and our imperfect natures must be accounted for in our dreams. I look forward to spending eternity in a new Eden, but for now I'm willing to revel in as much Ever After as possible with the woman of my dreams.

When Conflicts Arise

Conflict is inevitable, but combat is optional.
—Max Lucado

The process of striving together toward a common objective carries with it one of the most exciting opportunities to feel deeply connected as partners on an incredible journey. As most of us know well, however, working together has the potential to lead to significant conflict. The more challenging and taxing the project, the easier it is to bump or butt heads; at 2:00 A.M., with acres of screws remaining to be set, Jen and I shared some tense moments.

Many of us have had painful enough experiences in conflict with our spouse that we're gun-shy of being shot at again. Or perhaps we're willing to go back time and time again, but success is so unpredictable and unreliable. The good news: It is possible to navigate life's obstacles with skill and grace.

Conflicts are inevitable, even normal. Your buttons get pushed, there's a reaction, and you find yourself questioning whether the differences can be managed and overcome. You've taken the time to dream together and want to make the dreams a reality, but what do you do when once again you find yourself asking, "How do we get past this one?"

Of all the times I've had the thought *There is no humanly possible way for us to resolve this one and both feel good about it,* I've never been right! Back in chapter 5, I encouraged you toward operating effectively as teammates and adopting a no-losers policy. I now want to take a few moments for seven steps to a win/win solution that can help to bring the most out of your no-losers policy.

God's dream for your marriage is unity with each other and with him. As impossible as our conflicts may seem in the moment, he is devoted to helping couples stay "one" in spirit and purpose. Keep in mind that if you and your spouse are experiencing anything other than unity, something is blocking the Lord's access to you and your marriage. More than likely it's something either of you inadvertently placed there; attempting to figure out who's at fault in creating the division, instead of being reminded of God's overwhelming devotion to unity, is not profitable (John 17:6–26). If you agree together to allow him to help you become reconnected, he *will* assist in the process.

Step One: Commit to a No-Losers Policy

Remind yourselves that you're already teammates. You're joined together in the common goal and purpose of marriage, even if you're not yet connected on the specific issue. As teammates, you must bring to mind, over and over again, that in order for either to win—and thus for the team to win—you both must feel good about where you end up.

Commit to finding an alternative you both like. You'll find that defenses start dropping once you don't have to watch your back or worry about being strong-armed or sold on an idea. Take comfort in knowing that being one of the team's key members means you won't accept a solution unless it works for you too. This all goes a long way toward reestablishing a marriage's feeling of safety.

223

Step Two: Hear Each Other's Hearts

While using Heart Talk and the ICU model, take time to identify, care, and understand each other's feelings about the topic at hand. I can't overstress the importance of doing this. You'll have a far easier time working enthusiastically together as teammates with each knowing that your feelings matter and are regarded as important. You'll be astounded by how relaxed and cooperative you both will feel once you're understood and cared for. We also typically listen better once we feel listened to and understood.

Step Three: Pause, Pray, and Seek God

Actively include God in the process. Ideally you want to pray together and pray out loud, making sure that part of your prayer includes asking God to help you rediscover unity. This potentially serves two purposes. The first is allowing God to lead you, assuming that if he has an opinion on what you should do, it would be the best of all possible options. This places you in a position to transcend the limits of your own minds. Be aware of being cornered by your own perspectives, especially on an issue that's costly. It's easy to become negative and imagine that challenges are insurmountable. However, you can't fail when you allow an infinite Creator to open your minds to believe and act on *his* perspective. He wants to bring you into unity!

The second purpose of seeking God in your struggle is probably more important than having him provide a solution. The moment husband and wife come together to seek divine guidance, unity is instantly restored. Once again you'll be standing united as teammates instead of being squared off as adversaries. Still no solution, but you're looking for one together, as partners. In the midst of an impasse this is typically a welcome relief.

Step Four: Seek to Find a Win/Win Solution

From a place of unity, a couple is poised to begin actively searching for a win/win solution. In fact, numerous ways are available to find one. You may want to research possibilities, or perhaps consult with people who have related experience or special expertise. One of my favorites is to brainstorm for ideas—this can include agreeing to let your thoughts run wild and then writing down every possible idea that crosses your minds. Make it okay to suggest ideas that might even initially seem crazy or ridiculous. *Don't judge them, just write them down.* After you've assembled as long a list as you can, go back and begin evaluating each item. You'll be surprised at how this process opens doors to true creativity. The point is not to form an exhaustive list of potential solutions, but more to open your minds to possibility and creativity.

Step Five: Land on One You Both Like

Decide on a solution that works for both of you. Don't settle easily for something you don't really care for; because it's not a win if you don't like it, and it's hard to stay enthusiastic and committed to work out an option you're not excited about. Be careful about reducing your expectations. If in the end either one feels compromised, the solution is not a win for the individual, and therefore not a win for the team.

Step Six: Try It Out!
 Step Seven: Rework If Necessary

The last two steps in the process are simpler than simple: Give it a try—put the idea into practice—and then reevaluate and rework at any point where either of you don't like it. Again, remain flexible on this. Give each other grace; you're both changing and growing. As long as you're both committed to unity, and you remain available to allowing the Lord to work with you, few situations will arise that can't be overcome in a way that both parties fully embrace.

As a result of such ongoing investment in each other and in your marriage, your relationship will be strengthened. Your confidence in each other, in yourself, and in God will continue to grow, and the light of Christ will shine increasingly brighter through your relationship. You'll encounter hurdles along the way as you attempt to use a no-losers policy, but even those situations become powerful testimonies when overcome. The stories of how couples encounter, work through, and overcome life's inevitable challenges provide tremendous hope for those questioning whether it's even possible. Your story will provide a road map for those preparing to engage the journey.

Conclusion

As the old cliché describes, you can have "a bit of heaven here on earth" when you begin experiencing God's hand in the midst of discovering your ability to put into motion your hopes for a future of promise. Did you know your desire for eternal purpose and meaning are birthed in the heart of your Creator, that you can trust him with your deepest longings? Are you open to receiving God's permission to make your dreams a reality?

Your investment may come with immediate benefits, such as turning your fixer-upper into a warm sanctuary of safety, and with care it will pay dividends for years to come. Dreams will most assuredly be met with conflict and fear, but by nailing down the steps that take you there, you'll be empowered to clarify your vision and successfully negotiate any challenge you might encounter while sojourning toward your Ever After.

——————— *to* **Ponder** *and* **Discuss** ———————

1. Can you see ways in which our consumer-oriented society has encouraged you to approach your marriage as a place to get your needs met? Explain.

2. A great marriage requires investment. In what ways are you investing in your marriage? In what ways do you want to invest differently?

3. What would you like to see become different in your marriage in the next year?

4. In what ways would you like to be more like Jesus? How would this growth help you more successfully realize your dreams?

5. What would need to take place in your life for those qualities to be developed?

6. Is growth in your personal character and integrity worth investing in? If so, why?

7. What is one step you can envision yourself taking that would help you move toward one of your dreams for your marriage?

CHAPTER 11

—REFRESHING—
Becoming Playmates

We don't stop playing because we grow old;
we grow old because we stop playing.
—George Bernard Shaw

Between our own personal struggles, the challenges of those around us, and the sobering truth of a world in pain, life can at times begin to look bleak. If we're not careful, the whole business of living can leave us discouraged or just plain exhausted. We may feel great about what we're striving toward, but if our energy and enthusiasm become depleted, we're sunk. In *The Play Solution*, relationship experts Lauer and Lauer write, "You've heard it many times—perhaps too many times: 'You have to work at relationship.' That's true. Yet if a relationship is nothing but work, it's probably not really working for you."[1]

Fortunately, even in the midst of all that's difficult, there's a life force within us that longs for a spark of inspiration and creativity. We're tempted to despair, yet we yearn for hope. Our hearts break and our spirits cry, but we crave laughter. Sometimes we just need a break or vacation from the struggle, even a temporary respite to recharge our batteries. Yes, our work is important, but it's likewise important that we play and feel revived. If we've been traveling along a hot, dusty road for days, when we stumble upon the waterfall cascading into a pool of fresh water, we long to dive in and be refreshed.

Bob the Snorkel Nerd

Several years ago some friends of ours were planning a Caribbean marriage cruise for thirty couples on a privately chartered, 240-foot sailing clipper. They ended up with an extra spot and asked if Jenni and I would like to join them. How do you turn down an offer like that?! Large cruise liners have never overly interested me, but this sounded like a one-of-a-kind adventure. Having grown up in Southern California, I already had a love for the ocean; an island paradise sounded incredible. I'd always wanted to snorkel in tropical waters. I couldn't wait.

We began making our plans and preparing for the trip, which for me meant attending to one critical detail: Without my glasses I'm hopelessly blind. If I put on a regular underwater mask, everything is a blur. I heard I could get a prescription mask made; that became top priority. The next day, while I was talking about it with a friend at work, he got excited—his sister in Texas was an optometrist. He was sure she'd be able to make one for me, and with a killer deal on the price. This was perfect! I gave her all the details and felt a huge sense of relief that I had everything covered. The timing was close, but she'd seemed confident that the mask would be completed with days to spare.

As the date to leave drew near I still hadn't received the mask. I checked in with my friend twice and he assured me all was well. But the day before we left, he regretfully informed me that a mistake had been made and there was no way I'd have it on time. Here I was on my way to paradise to swim with some of the most amazing fish in the world, and I wouldn't be able to see a thing. I was devastated.

I tried not to let my disappointment ruin the trip, but when everyone hustled about preparing to snorkel for the first time, I began to get depressed. I couldn't bear the thought of being anchored right above a spectacular underwater display and totally missing out. My wife saw me becoming more and more disheartened. She's not one to stand by and let fate have its way. Awe-inspiring in moments of crisis, she became determined to find a solution.

Jenni began racking her brain to figure out some way to do the impossible. Suddenly she had an idea. "Bob, did you bring your spare set of glasses?"

I mumbled yes, and her eyes lit up. "I bet I could find a way to attach your lenses to the mask."

I imagine I made a face. "Thanks for the thought, but there's no way that'll work." Besides being a farfetched idea, I knew I'd look like a total dork! I've got my dignity to keep, after all. I wasn't willing to play along.

My pride still intact, I marched up to the deck, grabbed a mask and snorkel from the box, and jumped into the sparkling sea. Not only could I not see, in my blindness I floundered around until I bumped into an urchin and got stung. Ouch!

Back on deck, my ever-patient and sympathetic wife resisted the temptation to make a wisecrack about men being unwilling to stop and ask for directions. Instead, she gently took the mask and led me back to our cabin. She popped out the lenses from my spare glasses and informed me that she was going to fasten them to the inside of the mask with the sticky part of some waterproof Band-

Aids she'd had the foresight to bring in case of an emergency.

She used a tiny pair of fingernail scissors and painstakingly cut the sticky strips from the Band-Aids. Then, positioning my big fat lenses inside the mask, she adhered them. It looked pretty funky, but believe it or not she pulled it off. I put on the mask and looked around the room. I could see! I glanced in the mirror and immediately realized I'd been transformed from mild-mannered Bob into "Bob the Snorkel Nerd." All I needed to complete the ensemble was a shirt with a pocket protector full of pens. I puffed out my chest and embraced my new persona.

As Jenni and I swam together I was able to see all the incredible scenery, the color, and a vast array of sea life: parrotfish, angelfish, stingray, beautiful coral, and more. I may have been a snorkel dork, but no matter—*I could see.* Together we laughed about it throughout the cruise, and my attire provided more than a few chuckles for the other couples. Now, thanks to my wife, who in my eyes can conquer the world, I have unforgettable memories of the trip, of tropical moments together, and of laughter with friends. I also returned home to find a special package waiting for me: a free prescription mask.

Ever gone on vacation or a date or had another time in life when high hopes of fun and rejuvenation were jolted by life throwing you another curve? We know our batteries need recharging and we set out to make it happen, but the best-laid plans can unexpectedly turn into disappointment or even disaster. A wallet or purse disappears, illness strikes, an argument explodes, the hotel looks nothing like the glossy brochure . . . the list goes on. And it certainly doesn't require a vacation for something like this to happen.

I was well on my way to allowing circumstances to ruin or at least seriously dampen my opportunity to be refreshed and renewed on our tropical getaway. Yet my wife stepped in to save the day. What she did was far more than provide a way to see pretty fish.

Far beyond overcoming an obstacle, the way she changed our experience from a downer to a great memory had less to do with what she did than the spirit with which she did it. Jenni became playful, and eventually I joined in. Sharing a playful spirit and thus becoming "playmates" is one of the most important ingredients to keeping a marriage fresh and alive.

Play. It's Serious Business

Life begins as a quest of the child for the man
and ends as a journey by the man to rediscover the child.
—Laurens Van der Post

To get serious about wanting to learn how to play, let's look once again to the experts. Thomas Crum writes, in an article about the wisdom of children, "I used to be an expert on play—as a child. Somehow, in my mature adult role, I've started to suppress my playful instincts for fear they might discredit my maturity."[2] When most of us do stumble back into feelings of total freedom and joy, we give a satisfied sigh and say, "Ah, I feel like a kid again!"

You see, being an adult is great for getting things done and handling life's mature responsibilities, but grown-ups typically forget how to play well. When two married adults can make room in their relationship to play wholeheartedly with childlike abandon—while keeping an adult mindset safely nearby to assure that all necessary responsibilities get handled—their marriage remains fresh and their spirits stay young.

Have you recently stopped and watched children play together? They can become *wholly* absorbed in building a sand castle, drawing a picture, or playing house. Developmental psychologists have long referred to child's play as their "work," and I find this to be an interesting analogy. What if I engaged my life with the same spirit as a child with imagination? Is that really possible? Could my marriage be a place to "play," filled with lighthearted exploration? Indeed, many people discover that play allows them to fully engage in life every day and to absorb it like a child. As a result, their lives are richer and more energized.

Here, balance is the key. Without a balance between the serious and the playful, marriage can lean too heavily toward work *or* play. And we crave that balance. If it all becomes too solemn and sober, we eventually lose the joy of living. If our life is lived out as one big party, even the pursuit of pleasure eventually becomes empty. Both the serious and the playful can separately be motivating and energizing; together they are amazing. Each enhances the other.

So far I've presented some of the serious and the enjoyable aspects of marriage, but it's easy to miss the implied aspects of play because our definition tends to be too narrow and restrictive. Let's sharpen the focus a bit.

I'm continually on the lookout for carefree moments. I love to laugh, am often silly (or stupid, if you ask my kids), and love to make others smile and watch their eyes light up. In fact, my all-time favorite sound is the laughter of my children. With all of the seriousness this crazy world imposes on my family, building fun, laughter, and relaxation into our homes is critical to persevering through the hard times. This gives us a positive foundation of emotional well-being to stand upon when things get tough.

I find that many times the opportunities for fun are there for the taking but go unnoticed and, thus, get missed. You might be surprised at what I found playful in our "Bob the Snorkel Nerd" transformation. (I'll show you in just a few moments.) With its many faces, what constitutes play varies greatly from person to person. This chapter is about learning to recognize opportunities and how to creatively seize them so that you can be refreshed in a marriage filled with spontaneity and fun.

What Is Play?

Defining play is a difficult task. If you ask ten different people what they do for a good time you'll likely get ten different answers. What one person thinks is a blast, another might think is dull, or worse. For instance, do you think skydiving sounds fun? How about going to the opera? Do you like jigsaw puzzles? Discussing politics? Cleaning out the garage? Lying in the sun? The possibilities are endless.

Play can involve creativity—painting a picture, plotting a story, writing a song. It can come in a form of recreation like sports or camping. Your body might be fully engaged—e.g., snowboarding—or your mind primarily, as in reading a mystery. The activity can be as purposeful as solving a problem or as purposeless as a game of solitaire; as relaxed as a walk in the park or as energetic as mountain biking; as relaxing as tanning at the beach or as energizing as winning the World Series.

How many people view shopping as a form of entertainment? I guarantee the only thing I find enjoyable about shopping is speed and efficiency. One of my favorite shopping successes occurred when I had to get a new suit for my son's wedding. I have a defect in my closet that causes my clothes to shrink over time just by hanging there. From the time I pulled up in front of the shop to the time I left, including the process of selecting the suit, getting fitted, and buying a shirt and tie, only fifteen minutes had elapsed. I felt like I'd just set an Olympic record!

To congratulate myself, I asked the woman helping me if the speed of my purchase was unusual. She said it was actually fairly common . . . unless the guy brought his wife, and then it took four times longer. Go figure. I know plenty of people (well, yes, mostly women) who see shopping as a favorite pastime; the longer they take, the better it is.

The key to effective play (even if it's shopping!) has less to do with *what* we do and more to do with the *spirit* in which we do it.

If we approach a moment with a lighthearted attitude, many endeavors can become playful. In fact, playfulness can be an addition to activities and situations normally seen as everyday routine, like washing the car. The benefit: Playfulness adds a spark of energy to almost anything we do.

Play adds the element of enjoyment to our activities by pulling us toward being present in the moment. It may include a degree of spontaneity, creativity, humor, excitement, challenge, or silliness. A playful heart brings a measure of lightness, even in moments filled with seriousness. During our Intensives at NIM we take our clients' pain and struggle very seriously, but we also look for appropriate opportunities to hook their playful sides. We're engaged in the important work of helping couples on the brink of divorce find hope for their future together; wonderful moments of humor always lift our moods and allow us to relate as ordinary people. Most clients feel enormous relief as they rediscover their ability to laugh and play together.

Couple Play

Right in the midst of all that matters, now and forever, grand opportunities to play together as a couple are waiting to be discovered. Subtle forms of play lie beyond the more obvious varieties of recreation and games. The life missions we engage with hope of changing the world can all be accomplished with intense focus; often we take our call and responsibility to be a loyal steward of God's kingdom with complete seriousness. Yet if an individual can enjoy the spirit of adventure, creative energy is found in both the quest and the victory, followed by plenty of opportunity to revel in celebration! The process of getting to know one another can be handled with the sterile efficiency of a job interview—*or,* we can take hold of the thrill of it. In the romantic journey, playfulness awakens the senses to fascination and intrigue, culminating with the deep satisfaction of a warm embrace.

What's your prevailing mood when you are faced with new challenges? In the Caribbean, while I was getting more and more discouraged, Jenni was not only moved by my sadness, she was energized by the obstacle of my eyesight. My blindness to see possibilities was eclipsed by her clear vision for potential. Jen rarely meets a hill she's unwilling to scale. Her creative juices start to stir, and her mind opens up. In moments like these, her only limitations seem to come from the doubters, like me, who tell her it can't be done. This, of course, only serves to motivate her even more.

Once I was willing to get over my self-conscious pride I began to step into playful adventure with her. After all, what did we really have to lose? A few minutes that would never be missed anyway. But still I didn't plunge into the spirit of the moment; I eased in. Skeptically I watched her operate. Unlike me, Jenni was already fully engaged—she seems to more easily enter the "zone." She wasn't about to let small details stand between her and a potential once-in-a-lifetime opportunity.

As she worked through my dilemma, her focus was incredible. She determined exactly where on the mask each lens must be positioned. She carefully applied each tiny strip of tape and then tested it to make sure everything stayed secure. I found myself getting lost in the experience and began to cheer her on with the application of each sticky strip.

Within a short time I noticed my skepticism turning to admiration. I even stopped caring if it worked; I became caught up in the fun of trying. I knew that no matter how it all ended up, we had a great story in the making. The lunacy of it simply made for more fun. When I put on the mask and met Bob the Snorkel Nerd, my mind opened to the many ways I could play this to the hilt. Of course I had to share it with friends on the boat. They were all struck by Jenni's sheer ingenuity, and yes, they thought I looked like a complete goofball. But by the time we took the first test run, we had our own cheering section.

During my first swim Jenni kept tabs on how things were working. We shared notes on the mind-blowing sea life we saw together. And through it all my love and admiration for her grew to new heights. After my inaugural voyage, we all shared a time of celebration on the boat, and Jenni and I felt extremely close. I learned an awful lot about both of us. I was surprised to see how much my stubbornness and self-consciousness kept me at first from even entertaining the chance for a playful adventure. The contrast between Jenni's openness and my closed-ness was striking. I was only fully able to recognize how impossible I was being after stepping into the game with her and experiencing it firsthand.

Playful Tips

Fortunately, learning to become skilled at playing takes a lifetime. It's humanly impossible to exhaust the possibilities. I only know this theoretically, so feel free to spend the rest of your life trying to prove me wrong. There's so much to learn and so little time. Since the opportunities are vast and style is personal, the best I can offer are several ideas to help on your journey to master the serious art of playfulness . . . or is it the playful art of seriousness?

(1) Playfulness Is More Attitude Than Activity

Remember: You can bring a playful spirit to the table in most situations. Don't restrict yourself by holding too tightly to a narrow definition. Play doesn't have to be silly or competitive, and it doesn't have to be obvious. You can make a game out of almost anything. I engage the spirit of play in the serious endeavor of helping to save marriages by using all the creative energy I can muster to find new and more effective ways to serve people. Our team is engaged in a common pursuit, and we lock arms and strive together toward a meaningful goal. We work hard, we play along the way, and we laugh a lot. I keep learning new things about myself and how to steward the roles and responsibilities I've been given more effectively, and I make sure to enjoy the journey, keeping the spirit of play close at hand.

Even the mature act of sexual connection can lose its energy and vitality over time if we forget how to play together. Tina Tessina writes:

> The burden of passion can be a heavy one. Having to rev up the energy for a passionate, heavy-breathing session making love after a hard day's work can be an appalling prospect. How much more inviting it is to be able to have a silly giggle session, complete with sexual play, with the dearest person I know. Suddenly the heaviness and obligation are gone, and if I'm too tired to be passionate and alluring, I always seem to have the energy to "mess around."[3]

This is not meant in any way to dishonor the sacredness of a marital sexual union; instead, I want us to further consider the reach of a healthy balance between the serious and the playful. Jenni is my best friend *and* my lover.

(2) Be in the Moment

Great play is always firmly rooted in the present. You can be reminiscing about the past by telling stories and remembering good times, but the experience is now. When I share the snorkel-nerd story, the fun of reliving it is in bringing someone in the present into our imaginations in order to share something from the past. We both create our own personal movie in our minds' eye, but we're sharing it here and now. This is not the same as living in the past, which is a way to escape a present life that doesn't feel worth living. It's more about enhancing your life today by allowing your past, particularly the fun and inspiring times, to retain a special place.

Dreaming is, of course, filled with play. Much like reminiscing, *the pleasure of the experience is in imagining possibilities while enjoying it now.* It can even be in creating fantasy and fictional stories together. I vividly remember how when our children were little, night after night our two youngest, Becky and Nathan, would beg us to let them sleep in their older sister's room. Jessica had a gift; to the great delight of her younger siblings, she spontaneously created the most amazing stories about Matilda and Mr. Moose. Storytelling and playfully thinking about the future can include fact or fancy, as long as it's shared for the purpose of having fun. If the future-oriented activity is not done as lightheartedly as telling a story about Matilda and Mr. Moose, you're taken out of the moment and most likely are turning toward worry.

(3) Allow Your Play to Be Inspired

At its best, play is a heart-opening experience. When the doors to our hearts are open, the breath of God faithfully enters and we become inspired: "I stand at the door and knock. If anyone hears my voice and opens the door, I will come in" (Revelation 3:20). God not only wants our play to be inspired, he wants to be part of it. Clearly he wants us to approach life with an appreciation of the seriousness of it all. Yet we're our Father's children, and ultimately he created us for joy and laughter, fun and play. Do you think he gets any less joy out of hearing heartfelt belly chuckles and squeals of delight from his children than we do from ours?

The spirit of inspired play, and God's desire for our joy to be made complete, is wonderfully captured in the celebration of Psalm 126:

When the Lord brought back the captives to Zion, we were like men who dreamed. Our mouths were filled with laughter, our tongues with songs of joy. Then it was said among the nations, "The Lord has done great things for them." The Lord has done great things for us, and we are filled with joy. Restore our fortunes, O Lord, like streams in the Negev. Those who sow in tears will reap with songs of joy. He who goes out weeping, carrying seed to sow, will return with songs of joy, carrying sheaves with him. (vv. 1–6)

Allow God's Spirit to inhabit your play.

(4) Don't Take Yourself Too Seriously

One of the fastest ways I know to spoil a refreshing moment is by being unable or unwilling to laugh at myself. We're all imperfect, and we all make mistakes. Most of us genuinely try to do our best and still we blow it. We know that some of the most important learning involves a dose of trial and error. Can't we at least look to find some humor in it? This is significantly harder for those with people in their lives who've made it a point to regularly criticize, ridicule, or belittle. But, generally, in the presence of those we love who also love us, opportunities to laugh together about our common human weaknesses and mistakes abound.

One of my sisters is masterful at this. She can tell stories on herself better than anyone I know. When we were growing up she was particularly clumsy at times and had countless stories of falling down *and* up stairs, tripping over invisible objects, regularly doing and saying embarrassing things. She was always able to see the humor in her predicament and could weave a tale that left us all in stitches. Her stories would then encourage the rest of us to share ours.

(5) *Take Large Doses of Humor*

My friend and colleague Bob Burbee has done much to assist me in this writing process. He can tell wonderful stories, and some of my favorites include his parents, who've been married for fifty years. One of the healthiest elements of their relationship is their openness to humor. He says,

> My parents enjoy playing dominoes. It's one of the ways we all play together. During a recent game my mother became "tickled" by something my father said; the more she laughed, the more we all did, and soon we were gasping for air and holding our stomachs. I remarked to my father that something must be right about their relationship if after fifty years Mom still laughs at his goofy sense of humor.

When you laugh together, you're giving both yourself and your partner a marvelous dose of tonic.

Please don't confuse ridicule with humor. Ridicule is an expression of contempt and is a tool we use when we want to dominate the other. We may laugh at someone else's expense, but if they're not in on the joke or feel diminished by it, there is loss of relationship rather than enhancement. This may be the test of genuine humor versus ridicule: If the humor enhances relationship, then it's something shared; if not, it probably involves ridicule in some way.

By the way, did you know:

> The average kindergartner laughs three hundred times a day, while the average adult laughs seventeen times a day.[4]

(6) *Make It Safe*

As with almost everything, play is hard to enter into and enjoy if you don't feel safe. Did you know that children in impoverished, war-torn countries will still engage in play when the environment appears to them to be relatively safe, even if for only a moment? If the environment is not safe, children will instinctively seek safety.[5] Adults are no different. It's impossible to relax in an unsafe place or with an unsafe person. Again, play, an openhearted experience, requires a level of trust and vulnerability. When we feel unsafe, we tend to stay defensive and overly cautious, both of which hinder our ability to become free and relaxed enough to play well.

If I'm interested in finding new venues for fun with my spouse and the venture feels stalled, exploring how safe the relationship is for both of us is a good place to start. In order to fully let go and embrace the moment, we need to know we will not regret dropping our guard. Especially true in marriage, this applies to our physical, emotional, spiritual, and mental well-being.

This is not to suggest that we can't take risks together, because many types of interaction include stretching the limits. But Jenni needs to know she can trust me to be careful, responsible, and respectful. And I need to know this about her. We need to know we can move in and out of play at will. Jenni needs to have confidence that if she doesn't want to engage anymore, I'll stop and/or she can leave. If she fears being trapped or senses that I won't recognize her limits, she'll feel unsafe and any joy in the moment will be lost.

In your relationship, having an underlying spirit of love, care, kindness, and sensitivity lays a solid foundation upon which to create play. A great example of this is in my friendship with Greg Smalley. Greg comes from a family that believes Gary Chapman's five love languages was missing one; apparently, teasing and practical jokes was supposed to be the sixth. Now, I love a good tease, and Greg and I can go at it. But we're both completely confident that the other cares deeply. We each trust that at any point when either of us isn't having fun, the joking will stop. The other person and the relationship are always far more important than the game.

There's a more complicated version of both people needing to have fun that's common in marriage. Jenni and I now usually play freely, but for a long time she felt extremely uneasy allowing much to happen. For years she was afraid that if she engaged with me in teasing or wrestling, it would invariably find its way to becoming sexual, or I would by default assume it was an indication of sexual interest.

Because this was an area of ongoing miscommunication between us, she often avoided being involved at all. She longed to just relax and have nonsexual fun without *always* having to deal with all the other stuff. One impetus to change occurred when I took the time to understand what a burden this had become for her. As I made a point of caring about her feelings and concentrated on making our playfulness as enjoyable for her as it was for me, she became an enthusiastic participant.

(7) Planning to Play Can Be Fun Too

As much fun as recreation itself can be, planning fun can also make for a great time. As a guy I've often considered planning as preliminary to real play—something you just do or get through in order to enjoy the main event. I may have even enjoyed aspects of the planning, but I never looked at it as a form of pleasure until recently. Last year I was watching all the hoopla surrounding Jenni and our daughter, Becky, preparing for her senior prom. I couldn't get over how much time, attention, energy . . . and cash went into a two- or three-hour event. It reminded me of my older daughter Jessica's wedding, which also baffled me. Then, in an instant of revelation, the truth hit me. For my wife and daughters, some of the most enjoyable parts of the whole event actually may have been preparing for it!

When I share this insight, women enthusiastically agree. How could I be this old, having been around this many females for this many years, and never before understood this detail? It even began to make a little sense. Not that I've learned to enjoy getting ready for a night out, but I've begun to see opportunities for fun that I hadn't fully seized before.

Cultivating Playfulness

When husband and wife are fully engaged together in an activity, and both are being stimulated, it's a lot like playing together. Some couples can tackle a household project like redecorating, remodeling, or landscaping, and the relationship is enhanced by the project. Yet others approach a similar project and the activity leads to squabbling and conflict; in these couples, the project is not pleasurable but instead somehow brings out the worst in each of them. What's the difference?

Some differences we've already alluded to—for instance, safety, devotion, and a capacity to find humor in the activity—but there's probably another element too. Could it be that couples who find the project engaging are those who welcome the inherent challenge? They find stimulation in attempting something new together, or imagining the finished project motivates them to embrace the activity. The challenge allows them to test themselves in an ultimately satisfying way. It may be difficult or even stressful, and it might entail tons of work. But the effort is worthwhile when both can aim together at a rewarding accomplishment they would not have had otherwise.

As an example of how this can work, let me describe a "play" activity Mary Jo and Bob Burbee share together. They enjoy entertaining people in their home. In planning a party or get-together with friends or family, they sometimes get lost for hours in brainstorming what could be fun. Bob and Mary Jo generate ideas and then evaluate whether their resources can meet their objectives for the event. Part of the planning is negotiating tasks and responsibilities they'll each do to pull it off. Bob loves to cook, so he usually gets the chef's hat. Mary Jo enjoys decorating and details not associated with the cooking. Bob notes,

> When the event is over, we both feel a deep satisfaction about what took place and the fun we had in pulling it off. We may spend considerable time reviewing the event and sharing ideas about the next party so we can improve on the party we just had. The experience is stimulating for both of us, and there is a sense of accomplishing something important to both of us.

Available to you are myriad ways to cultivate more drama in marriage. You're only limited by your own imagination. I hope the insights in this chapter are of some use, but either way the idea here is to stir up interest and understanding about how play does or doesn't happen in your marriage. The suggestions should both affirm you and show you areas for growth.

"What if our relationship is devoid of play entirely?" If this is how you're feeling, your biggest challenge may lie not in how to start engaging but in whether you're willing to consider the prospect at all. Remember: It's in our nature to be refreshed, so if that's not occurring, most likely you and your spouse are either blocking yourselves from it or have committed in some way not to experience it. You may even have good reasons for not opening yourself up to interaction.

The point is, if we're not receptive to play, nothing is likely to entice us into enjoying ourselves while we're kicking and screaming and trying to get away. No one can be forced to perform, and I'm not sure you can really force yourself to play either. But it may be possible to position and orient yourself in such a way that it could happen. You might need to start slow, but each refreshing moment becomes a building block to more lighthearted fun, and after a while it becomes easier and easier to enter in. Because play is fun, it's inherently rewarding.

Even after a rough start and several near-failures, Jenni is my journeying partner in a divinely inspired adventure, an endless source of fascination in our romantic love story, *and* she is my all-time favorite playmate.

Conclusion

Refresh. Isn't it a brilliant word? The best part about it is that God designed a blueprint for us to ensure we would be refreshed. Have you ever looked throughout Scripture at all the places he instructs us to rest, to worship, to be in fellowship? He calls this (in English) *Sabbath.* Your marriage needs to be a place where you can go to recharge your batteries. When you play together, you give your bodies and souls a respite from the tensions and stresses of everyday living. Our Maker knew we'd have a hard time giving ourselves permission to be revived, so he commanded us to do so. If life feels like traveling along a hot, dusty road, it's time to find a waterfall of fun. Dive in and be refreshed.

A Final Word

In his book of daily mediations titled *Listening to Your Life,* novelist, essayist, and preacher Frederick Buechner describes how one day, while attending church in New York, the words of preacher George Buttrick touched him deeply. "One particular sermon with one particular phrase" stayed with Buechner until he wrote about it some twenty-five years later.

> Jesus Christ refused the crown that Satan offered him in the wilderness, Buttrick said, but he is king nonetheless

because again and again he is crowned in the hearts of the people who believe in him. And that inward coronation takes place, Buttrick said, "among confession, and tears, and great laughter."[6]

In these words Buechner found truth that had been missing in his life. What proved to be a monumental breakthrough for him is at the crux of our journey here. Is it possible that the Ever After we seek is most readily found in the heartfelt confession of our love to one another—our confessions of hopes, fears, and desires? And yes, of our sorrow for past hurts? Do we want to glorify our Lord with our marriage? Surely Christ is crowned with our longing for him and each other, his glory reflected in our tears . . . and our *great* laughter.

We never tire of the epic tale of undying love between a man and a woman, spun with timeless threads of adventure and romance. Our imagination is captured by chronicles wrought with danger and uncertainty, where two lovers dare to encounter their greatest fears for the sake of the other. Why? *Theirs is a love worthy of gallant sacrifice, a story worth living.*

Such a love story may sound like fantasy, but it is one birthed in the beginnings of our very own—the story we're living right now. What we'd come to believe as being merely fantasy is, in fact, our deepest reality.

My prayer for you today, dear reader . . . is that this will be your "Once upon a time. . . ."

———————— *to* P o n d e r *and* D i s c u s s ————————

1. Do you personally tend to have a more serious or playful outlook on life? Have you always been that way?

2. Do you lean more toward play or work? Has it ever been out of balance, and what was the impact on your marriage?

3. Have you experienced a time on vacation, or some other time, when you had high hopes of fun and rejuvenation only to be disappointed?

4. Do you typically experience your marriage as more serious or playful? Do you like it the way it is, or would you prefer it to be different, and, if different, how?

5. What are some of the ways you have played together as a couple? Do you both enjoy the same kinds of play, or different?

6. Describe the last project or endeavor you and your spouse tackled together. Did you go into the project with a more serious or playful attitude?

7. In what ways did Jesus display playfulness, and how can you apply his example to your marriage?

8. How has this book inspired you to live differently?

ENDNOTES

INTRODUCTION

1. Dr. Greg Smalley and Dr. Robert S. Paul, *The DNA of Relationships for Couples* (Wheaton, IL: Tyndale, 2006).

CHAPTER 1

1. D. Mace and R. Mace, *Enriching Marriages: The Foundation Stone of Family Strength.* Cited in N. Stinnett, B. Chesser, J. DeFrain, and P. Knaub (eds.), *Family Strengths: Positive Models for Family Life* (Lincoln, NE: University of Nebraska Press, 1980), 197–215.
2. *Webster's New World College Dictionary,* 3rd edition (New York: Simon & Schuster/Macmillan, 1997).

CHAPTER 3

1. Ravi Zacharias, *Recapture the Wonder* (Nashville: Integrity, 2003), 13.
2. Bill Ewing, *Rest Assured* (Rapid City, South Dakota: Real Life Press, 2003), 248–49.

CHAPTER 4

1. John Eldredge, *Wild at Heart* (Nashville: Thomas Nelson, 2001).
2. John and Stasi Eldredge, *Captivating* (Nashville: Thomas Nelson, 2005).

CHAPTER 5

1. Dr. Gary Smalley, Dr. Greg Smalley, Michael Smalley, and Dr. Robert S. Paul, *The DNA of Relationships* (Wheaton, IL: Tyndale, 2004).
2. Dr. Greg Smalley and Dr. Robert S. Paul, *The DNA of Relationships for Couples* (Wheaton, IL: Tyndale, 2006).

CHAPTER 6

1. Stephen R. Graves and Thomas G. Addington, *Behind the Bottom Line: Powering Business Life With Spiritual Wisdom* (San Francisco: Jossey-Bass, 2002), 83.

CHAPTER 7

1. Gary Chapman, *The Five Love Languages* (Chicago, IL: Northfield Publishing, 1992).

CHAPTER 8

1. Dr. Gary Sweeten, Dave Ping, and Anne Clippard, *Listening for Heaven's Sake* (Cincinnati: Teleios, 1999), 84.

CHAPTER 9

1. Source unknown. Emphasis added.

CHAPTER 10

1. Steven R. Covey, *The Seven Habits of Highly Effective People* (New York: Simon and Schuster, 1989).

CHAPTER 11

1. Jeanette Lauer, PhD, and Robert Lauer, PhD, *The Play Solution* (Chicago: Contemporary, 2002), n.p.
2. Thomas Crum, "Learning From the Experts: The Playful Wisdom of Children" in *In Context: A Quarterly of Sustainable Culture* (Spring 1986:13): 17.
3. Tina Tessina, "It's a Dirty Job: The Silly Solution for Healthy Relationships" in *In Context: A Quarterly of Sustainable Culture* (Spring 1986:13): 35.
4. M. Sayer Saunders and A. Goodale, "The Relationship Between Playfulness and Coping in Preschool Children" in *American Journal of Occupational Therapy* (March/April 1999): 221–26.
5. Lauer and Lauer, n. p.
6. Frederick Buechner, *Listening to Your Life* (New York: HarperCollins, 1992), 23–24.

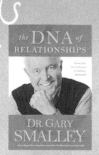

Building, Renewing and Restoring the Promise of a Great Marriage

NATIONAL INSTITUTE of MARRIAGE

The DNA of Relationships Book

Have you ever felt as if you're... REPEATING THE SAME MISTAKES IN YOUR RELATIONSHIPS? The founder of the NIM Intensive program, Dr. Robert S. Paul, along with Dr. Gary Smalley, Dr. Greg Smalley and Michael Smalley illustrate the DNA of relationships, showing how each one of us is uniquely designed for healthy relationships with friends, family, and coworkers. You don't have to live with dysfunctional relationships anymore! Understanding how you are designed will start you on a journey to healthy and enjoyable relationships.

Order at nationalmarriage.com

The DNA of Relationships for Couples Book

Dr. Robert Paul shows readers who are struggling in their marriage the steps to take to strengthen and rebuild their marriage relationship in one of our outstanding resources, The DNA of Relationships for Couples. The practical solutions are built on the basic steps that are explained in The DNA of Relationships. Dr. Robert Paul and Dr. Greg Smalley use fictional couples (based on real client experience) who are grappling with real-life problems ranging from work and family priority balance issues to extramarital affairs. Through the telling of the stories of real couples going through the step-by-step counseling process, the book provides a tool to help both partners identify destructive relationship habits and explains how to begin the rebuilding process.

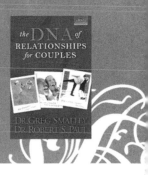

Order at nationalmarriage.com

The DNA of Relationships for Couples Conference

Over time, our talented team has translated the principles from our Intensive Marriage Counseling into the life-changing DNA of Relationships for Couples Conference. Designed to enrich all marriages, even great ones, this conference will be a benefit to you and your community.

Order at nationalmarriage.com

The DNA of Relationships for Couples Small Group Resources

Based on NIM's highly acclaimed DNA of Relationships for Couples Conference, this small group resource is unlike any other. Featuring all six sessions of the conference on individual DVDs, 12 Conference Manuals, a copy of the DNA of Relationships for Couples book and a promotional DVD.

Order at nationalmarriage.com

NATIONAL INSTITUTE of MARRIAGE

www.nationalmarriage.com